Making Big Data Work for Your Business

A guide to effective Big Data analytics

Sudhi Sinha

Impackt Publishing
We Mean Business

Making Big Data Work for Your Business

First published: October 2014

Production reference: 1221014

Published by Impackt Publishing Ltd.
Livery Place
35 Livery Street
Birmingham B3 2PB, UK.

ISBN 978-1-78300-098-2

www.impacktpub.com

Credits

Author

Sudhi Sinha

Reviewers

Vikash Gaur

Richard Heimann

Acquisition Editor

Richard Gall

Content Development Editor

Sweny Sukumaran

Copy Editors

Tanvi Bhatt

Simran Bhogal

Karuna Narayanan

Alfida Paiva

Faisal Siddiqui

Project Coordinator

Venitha Cutinho

Proofreaders

Simran Bhogal

Maria Gould

Ameesha Green

Paul Hindle

Graphics

Ronak Dhruv

Abhinash Sahu

Production Coordinator

Melwyn D'sa

Cover Work

Simon Cardew

Foreword

Big Data is now ubiquitous. At its core, the Big Data phenomenon includes a realization, a vision, and a resulting implementation effort. There is now a widespread realization (indeed, one may even say that an inflection point has been reached) that data can hugely benefit applications in virtually all corners of society. This has given rise to the vision of a data-driven world, one in which organizations, governments, disciplines, communities, and individuals alike try to capture as much data as possible and then use knowledge gleaned from the data to make decisions. The race is therefore on to implement this vision, with needs for ever more tools to capture data, for distributed and parallel platforms to process huge volumes of data, and for analytics software to glean the available insights.

And there is more to come. Looking forward, just over the horizon, the Internet of Things is emerging. On this Internet, ordinary appliances such as refrigerators, thermostats, furnaces, and cars have sensors that allow them to generate torrents of data and to communicate with one another. Companies are eager to build this Internet, as it will allow them to offer high-margin, value-added services, projected to be worth billions of dollars. When this Internet takes hold, it will make the data-driven world even bigger and the data deluge even more ubiquitous.

Thus, it is no wonder that companies are racing to prepare themselves for the Big Data era and the coming Internet of Things. It is difficult, however, to know exactly where to start and what to do. This is where this book comes in. Written by Sudhi Sinha at Johnson Controls, with decades of experience in data management, this is a perfect starter book for any manager who wants to understand and explore Big Data. The book covers important challenges, ranging from building an overall strategy, to creating new opportunities, to managing projects, and to driving Big Data communications effectively throughout the entire organization. The book is peppered with concrete examples and practical tips, in an engaging presentation style. The Big Data field is evolving quickly, and this book serves as a quick and practical introduction to the field. I have found it very informative and interesting, and I believe that you will too.

AnHai Doan
Professor, University of Wisconsin-Madison, and Chief Scientist, WalmartLabs, USA

About the Author

 **Sudhi Sinha** is a business leader with over 17 years of global experience in technology and general management. He started his career designing and developing database management systems and business intelligence systems. Currently, he is the Vice President for product development and engineering for Building Technology and Services in Johnson Controls. He is also responsible for several Big Data initiatives. He has worked in technology consulting, engineering, sales, strategy, operations, and P&L roles across US, Asia, and Europe. He has written extensively on various technical and management topics including applying Big Data to different aspects of business. Sudhi holds a degree in Production Engineering from Jadavpur University, Kolkata, India. He resides in Mumbai with his wife, Sohini who is an entrepreneur and a fashion designer.

Acknowledgments

I have been incredibly lucky to have always worked with exceptional people and be given the right opportunities. First, I want to thank Mr. N. Chandrasekaran, CEO of Tata Consultancy Services, who helped me crystallize my thinking on various aspects of technology and management for the past 7 years. Chandra has always encouraged me to think carefully about any subject at hand and do extensive background research. I tried to follow this advice while developing this book.

Next, I want to express my sincerest thanks to Mr. Soren Bjerg, VP and Managing Director, Building Efficiency (Asia), Johnson Controls, and Mr. Swarup Biswas, VP of Asia Lines of Business, Building Efficiency, Johnson Controls for letting me cut my teeth in Big Data initiatives. Without the education and coaching from Mr. Howard Hayes, VP of Data and Analytics and Dr. Youngchoon Park, Director of Data and Analytics, both working for Johnson Controls, all that I know about Big Data would not have been possible. They helped me navigate the complex and evolving world of Big Data and develop many of the frameworks and topics discussed in this book. They introduced me to leading thinkers such as Prof. AnNhai Doan and Prof. Jignesh Patel of University of Wisconsin at Madison who have guided me on many topics that are technical as well as managerial.

I would also like to thank the one whom I consider as my guru in Big Data—Prof. Victor Myer-Scoenberger of University of Oxford; his book on Big Data opened my eyes for the first time and has had the deepest influence on my thinking around Big Data. I thank Joel Makower of GreenBiz for the many interactions we had on the scope of Big Data in energy and sustainability, and for publishing many of my early articles.

Finally, this book would not have been possible without the untiring efforts and patience of my editors Richard Gall and Sweny Sukumaran, project coordinator Venitha Cutinho, and the other people at Packt Publishing who worked through the various stages of this book.

About the Reviewers

Vikash Gaur is Assistant Vice President with Cognizant's Manufacturing & Logistics Practice heading delivery for its North America customers. He drives growth for his unit, ensures flawless delivery of leading-edge technology projects for global customers, while building future-proof solutions that ensure market leadership few years into the future.

Vikash is a management professional with almost 20 years of business and technology experience in leadership positions. He has played a variety of roles in the manufacturing industry and in IT, beginning with the automotive industry and moving on to IT services in the manufacturing industry.

He has experience in business consulting, business process re-engineering, program management, solution architecting, business-IT alignment, and leadership development. With his unerring ability to understand the real challenges that customers face, he helps make customers' businesses stronger, often leveraging emerging technologies.

Richard Heimann is Chief Data Scientist at L-3 National Security Solutions (NSS) (NYSE:LLL) and is an EMC Certified Data Scientist with concentrations in spatial statistics, data mining, Big Data, and pattern discovery and recognition. Richard also leads the Data Science team at the L-3 Data Tactics Business Unit. L-3 NSS and L-3 Data Tactics are both premier Big Data and Analytics service providers based in Washington D.C. and serve customers globally.

Richard is an adjunct professor at University of Maryland, Baltimore County, where he teaches Spatial Analysis and Statistical Reasoning. Additionally, he is an instructor at George Mason University, teaching Human Terrain Analysis and is also a selection committee member for the 2014-2015 AAAS Big Data and Analytics Fellowship Program and member of the Washington Exec Big Data Council.

Richard has also recently published a book titled *Social Media Mining with R, Packt Publishing*. He has recently supported DARPA, DHS, the US Army, and the Pentagon with analytical support.

To my parents Mr. Sukumar Ranjan Sinha and Mrs. Keya Sinha who not only brought me into this world and taught me a lot, they also loved me and encouraged me for all the good things that I have been associated with including this book.

And to my lovely wife Sohini, who showered me with her love, encouragement, and patience while I was working on this book.

"Data is the only perpetual entity. Actions and human interventions have definitive outcomes and a definitive life however long. Data lives forever and takes a new evolving meaning."

Contents

Chapter 3: Managing Your Big Data Projects Effectively 39

Chapter 4: Building the Right Technology Landscape   57

Chapter 5: Building a Winning Team   79

Preface

In the 2008 historic presidential election in the United States, President Barack Obama captured the imagination of the nation with his *"Yes we can"* slogan and his different but definitive ideas. He employed social media very well to get his message out to the millions of new voters. Fast forward to 2012; he was facing a very difficult re-election campaign. This time he employed data and analytics to win this election. In his November 16, 2012 article in *The Atlantic*, Alexis Madrigal captures this transformative experimentation in details. For the first time in history, a political campaign had a Chief Technology Officer in Harper Reed. Mr. Reed assembled an eclectic team from Google, Facebook, Twitter, and many other new age technology companies and initiated the project Narwahl. They mined through huge volumes of data—demographic, past voting patterns, economic data, social media interactions, and others to predict how the campaign is going to perform in each seat and how they can persuade individual voters. Big Data is here and now.

In the past 50 years, the world has seen itself transforming to the era of the information age; in the last 5 years, we have seen ourselves gravitating towards the Big Data age. Big Data touches every aspect of our lives. Talking about Big Data, we often refer to huge volumes, variety, and velocity of data—lots of data, different types of data, and data getting created, captured, and processed at breakneck speeds. We often use examples of the 1 billion plus Facebook users, the 3 billion plus likes they click on every day, the 100 billion credit card transactions that happen across the world, the millions of transactions that occur in individual retail chains every hour, the 200 million + e-mails sent every minute, and so on. Sometimes it is difficult for us to fathom the quantum of data.

Let me share an excellent representation that I saw in one of the infographics published by EMC (http://www.emc.com/campaign/global/big-data/hfbd-infographic-4web-1500.jpg). Data is measured in bytes or multiples of that. In the following table, we compare these multiples with more physical equivalents of words/pictures and sand:

Data	Numerical representation	Words/pictures	Sand
Byte	1	Single character	One grain of sand
Kilobyte	1,000	A sentence	Couple of pinches of sand
Megabyte	1,000,000	A 20 slide PowerPoint	Tablespoon of sand
Gigabyte	1,000,000,000	Ten yards of books on a shelf	Shoebox full of sand
Terabyte	1,000,000,000,000	300 hours of good quality video	Playground sized sandbox

Data	Numerical representation	Words/pictures	Sand
Petabyte	1,000,000,000,000,000	350,000 digital pictures	Sand on a mile long beach
Exabyte	1,000,000,000,000,000,000	100,000 times all the printed material in the Library of Congress	Sand on a beach from Miami to North Carolina
Zettabyte	1,000,000,000,000,000,000,000	Difficult to get an example	Sand on all the coastlines across the world

Traditional technologies have demonstrated limitations when the volume goes beyond a few terabytes. The new reality is terabytes of data are not considered enough to capture every transaction that happens in organizations or businesses in a year. Research group SINTEF published in their May 2013 report that 90 percent of the world's data was created in the past 2 years. In their 2011 Digital Universe Study, IDC has projected growth of information generated to be 50 times of current rate by 2020. Last year the global mobile data traffic is expected to be close to 1 Exabyte per month. So we see massive proliferation of Big Data everywhere every day.

Big Data not only relates to the new age technology companies, large financial institutions, or the mega retail chains; it also relates to traditional manufacturing companies and brick and mortar industries like construction. Today, a medium size building of 10,000 square meters generates over 10 gigabytes of data every year! Everybody is in awe of the size of data and the possibilities it brings. In the last few years, the companies have been scrambling to make sense of this type of Big Data and effectively use this to create new products and services to differentiate themselves and transform their businesses. Billions of dollars are getting invested worldwide in Big Data and trillions of dollars' worth of benefits are expected to be generated from them.

New disciplines of technology like Near Field Communications, Augmented Reality, and many others are getting enabled and impacted by Big Data. New economic models like Bitcoins are getting introduced because of the processing power unleashed by Big Data. Big Data is changing everything—the way we work, the way we live, and the way we interact with each other.

Not everybody has tasted success in pursuit of Big Data. While some companies experienced phenomenal success in adapting Big Data for their business, many others are still tentative and not sure how to pursue this space. There are many reasons for limited success or apprehension:

➤ Big Data is not only about technology, there needs to be a larger enabling ecosystem and the program needs to be integrated into the DNA of the business. There is limited assistance available on how to do that.

➤ There is a dearth of qualified and experienced people in different aspects of Big Data.

> ➤ There are very few successful established business models to create new value or unlock untapped potential across various industry verticals.

> ➤ When analytics supported by Big Data challenges many of the conventional practices and beliefs, a number of managers find it difficult to accept these new insights and act upon them. After all, they are influenced by over 50 years of evolution of management practices and models.

> ➤ Sometimes people equate Big Data to a specific technology application without understanding the complete stack, thereby limiting the possibilities of what can be leveraged or how to apply the different capabilities.

> ➤ There is clear acknowledgement today that we need a more holistic approach to and understanding of Big Data to use it effectively.

What this book covers

The technology for Big Data is evolving at a very rapid pace. You can access the new advancements easily and inexpensively. On the other hand, Big Data is fundamentally changing many paradigms of how we manage and grow businesses. Unfortunately, unlike many other disciplines, there is not enough guidance available on how to best leverage all of these new capabilities. This book is an attempt to address that space. This book also makes an attempt to tackle some of the limiting factors in the adoption of Big Data from amongst the points we discussed above.

In this book we will cover 8 different aspects of Big Data and how to be most effective in them.

Chapter 1, Building Your Strategy Framework, focuses on helping you map a path for yourself to make a big impact in your business using Big Data. This chapter helps you put a strategic context to Big Data and introduces a few tools to develop strategies, align existing ones, and cascade your new strategies across the organization.

Chapter 2, Creating an Opportunity Landscape and Collecting Your Gold Coins, deals with identifying and structuring specific initiatives around Big Data. This chapter introduces you to an approach of crafting Big Data projects as gold coins—identifying the gold coins, assessing their value, prioritizing them, and finally building a gold mine for greater organizational value by putting together all the gold coins.

Chapter 3, Managing Your Big Data Projects Effectively, starts with understanding how Big Data projects are different from other types of technology-intensive business transformation initiatives. It then helps you create a new project management framework Explore Validate Amplify better suited for Big Data projects, defining success criteria and management methodologies to deploy this framework. Finally, it provides guidance on how to handle different types of Big Data initiatives.

Chapter 4, Building the Right Technology Landscape, helps you understand the various technology layers and choices around Big Data and how they have evolved. This chapter helps you understand the differences between Big Data initiatives and massive data warehousing projects that people often get confused about. In this chapter, you are provided with some guidance on designing storage for Big Data and selecting the right technology for the various layers described.

Chapter 5, Building a Winning Team, introduces you to the various skills and the 6 different profiles required in your project's team to effectively implement various Big Data initiatives. This chapter also helps you identify where to source people for your Big Data projects, how to organize them, how to manage and motivate them, how to leverage external resources, and develop organizational capability for future needs.

Chapter 6, Managing Investments and Monetization of Data, deals with financial aspects around Big Data. It focuses on two important topics—valuation and monetization of data, and investment management of Big Data initiatives. The tools and techniques in this chapter will help you maximize your investments and unlock untapped value from your business.

Chapter 7, Driving Change Effectively, helps you increase the sustainability of business benefits brought about by Big Data through effective change management practices. This chapter helps you understand the major changes that are caused by Big Data and their significance for your business. This chapter also introduces you to a new change management framework called **IMMERSE** and how to deploy it. Finally, this chapter helps you develop a guiding coalition to drive change in your organization.

Chapter 8, Driving Communication Effectively, starts with identifying the need for increased communication around Big Data. It helps you identify your communication needs for various audiences, understand the various communication channels available and determine which ones are the most appropriate ones for those audience groups, build a communication plan, and manage the communication deployment. This chapter introduces you the TALK model to make communication effective.

This is a *how-to* book, designed and developed to help you implement some of the concepts in a very practical manner. It is therefore filled with examples from many walks of business. For many of these concepts and practices, there is no well-established precedence, so you will be introduced to many new frameworks and models.

Who this book is for

This book is intended for all the current and prospective practitioners of Big Data. This book is ideal if you are:

➤ Leading a Big Data initiative for your business or are thinking about starting one

➤ Part of the executive management team of a business and want to explore what this new craze around Big Data can do for your business

> A technology expert in the space of data and analytics who wants to become more effective in adding value to your business through better adoption of Big Data

> Part of a team that is struggling with using Big Data in your business

> A student who sees this as a potential career option

> A consultant who wants to help clients make more effective use of Big Data

> An industry analyst who wants to understand what makes one successful in pursuing Big Data

> An investor with companies that you think can make a big difference to its performance using Big Data

Every business of all sizes has equal opportunities with Big Data. This book is as much for people who work in or work for large companies, as much it is for people engaged with smaller businesses.

Peter Drucker made these now famous remarks, *culture eats strategy for breakfast*. To be effective in future, we need a culture of Big Data in our businesses. We hope this book will help you create that culture for your business.

Conventions

In this book, you will find a number of styles of text that distinguish between different kinds of information. Here are some examples of these styles, and an explanation of their meaning.

New terms and **important words** are shown in bold.

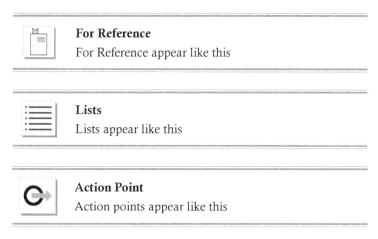

For Reference

For Reference appear like this

Lists

Lists appear like this

Action Point

Action points appear like this

Make a Note

Warnings or important notes appear in a box like this.

Tip

Tips and tricks appear like this.

Reader feedback

Feedback from our readers is always welcome. Let us know what you think about this book—what you liked or may have disliked. Reader feedback is important for us to develop titles that you really get the most out of.

To send us general feedback, simply send an e-mail to `feedback@impacktpub.com`, and mention the book title via the subject of your message.

Piracy

Piracy of copyrighted material on the Internet is an ongoing problem across all media. At Packt, we take the protection of our copyright and licenses very seriously. If you come across any illegal copies of our works, in any form, on the Internet, please provide us with the location address or website name immediately so that we can pursue a remedy.

Please contact us at `copyright@impacktpub.com` with a link to the suspected pirated material.

We appreciate your help in protecting our authors, and our ability to bring you valuable content.

1

Building Your Strategy Framework

Big data has clearly got everybody's attention, from academia to industry. Conservative estimates put the market of big data technologies to nearly 2 billion dollars in 2013. Research Company IDC expects this market to be in excess of 25 billion dollars by 2016. Even more interestingly, GE executives Peter Evans and Marco Annunziata believe that big data will influence over 10 trillion dollars worth of economic benefits to the global economy in less than 2 decades. Every major corporation with interest in this space is setting up multi-million dollar research initiatives with leading institutes and think-tanks.

Big data is radically transforming the way businesses are designed and operate. Now, your business can make sense of a huge volume, velocity, variety, variability of data, and effectively visualize the analysis of this data. Now, you do not have to spend hundreds of millions of dollars or years to get these types of capabilities. Technologies that enable organizations to make sense of big data are significantly reducing the entry barriers for such investments. These new capabilities are fundamentally altering many management practices and impacting all types of companies—small and big, traditional, and new age. Now, start-up companies can offer new insights into customer analytics to large retailers and become multi-million dollar organizations in little or no time. Similarly, traditional large manufacturing companies are focusing on more profitable service segments of their businesses derived from new insights around data and analytics.

Companies today are struggling with figuring out how to take the capabilities and possibilities from one-off initiatives that impact one or some parts of the business to broader usage. Executives are not questioning the value of masses of data; the question in their minds today is how to use it well and amplify its effects. They key lies in weaving big data into the strategic framework of your organization.

Using Big Data analytics to identify where to play and how to win, to grow your business

Often, organizational strategies evolve around entrenched perceptions; trends identified through sampling and organizational aspirations. Past performances and future prospects play a key role in this process. Organizations consider macro-economic environments, market trends, industry growth, competitive actions, core capabilities and adjacencies, and finally shareholder expectations in building their business strategy. In the past, such an approach has been able to keep pace with the evolution of various forces that have an impact on an organization's performance. Today, the rate of innovation, interventions, and insights around their current and future impact outpaces many other factors that impact the long-term or even medium-term sustainability of an organization's growth and profitability. Businesses need agility to respond to such challenges. Big companies sometimes get pulled back by their size and momentum; smaller companies sometimes lack the resources and reach to invest in response.

Building strategies around big data analytics is about finding value in data, and it is about enabling value through data. The following are seven simple steps that will help you do this:

> ➤ Understanding the changing landscape
> ➤ Identifying the strategic implications
> ➤ Spotting and simulating the growing influences
> ➤ Integrating new possibilities into planning
> ➤ Developing strategies
> ➤ Aligning existing initiatives
> ➤ Cascading your strategy

Throughout this chapter, I'll take you through each stage to ensure that your big data strategy is closely tied to your organization's strategy, which in turn will ensure that you are able to get the most from your data.

However, before we proceed further, it's a good idea to compile a list of various sources of revenue or various areas of key operations for your organization in a business catalog. For each of the revenue sources or operation areas, briefly capture how the company makes money from them and what the fundamental components of their operation are. This acts as a good compass for you to put some of the upcoming discussions in this and future chapters into context. It could be in a very simple manner as follows:

Business Catalog	Remarks
Product sales through direct sales	The company makes money through strategic pricing applied to differentiated solutions for different customer segments.
Product sales through channel partners	The company makes money through commission. Effective channel development and management (making it easy to do business with channel partners), marketing promotions to attract mass market customers, and achieving high volume turnovers is integral to making more money.
Technical maintenance services for directly sold products/solutions	The company makes money through higher returns in replacement parts, value added services, and labor hours.
Design services	The company makes money by helping customers design their implementation of your company's products, and services that they would normally outsource to a third party.

Understanding the changing landscape

The first step towards interlacing big data analytics into your organization's strategic framework is to understand how big data is changing the backdrop in which your company operates. This requires a shift in mindset. We are attuned to think of a changing landscape in terms of actions and outcomes. We have been trained that knowledge is power; we have been taught that history never repeats itself. However, these beliefs are no longer considered as absolute truths. Traditional strategic analysis techniques relied heavily on causality. Our core competencies revolved around what we can do, what we are good at, and what our reach is. Capabilities around what we know, what more we can find out, how we can connect the dots around such information, and how we can use these insights to change the business have not been generally considered core competencies. That is, until the advent of big data.

Imagine you have a service that helps travelers book hotel rooms and rent cars. You will have systems and capabilities to understand inventory movement in hotels in your network, possibly in other networks as well. You will also have ways to auction new bids from your travelers, and it is also likely that you will be able to adapt according to specific events, seasonality, and past data to arrive at price recommendations for both hotels as well as travelers.

Now, imagine if someone were able to modulate your hotel room pricing strategy with changes in plane ticket booking data. This could change the dynamics completely and give that person more opportunities for early profitable pricing and increased customer traffic.

In another example, consider yourself as the manufacturer of household or light commercial electronics goods, say, an industrial grade water purifier. You are probably using lot of data based on:

> ➤ **Customer segmentation**: How your customers are categorized into various demographic groups with different buying patterns

> ➤ **Pricing strategies**: How you sell your products at different price points for different markets or different sales channels

> ➤ **Component or finished product sourcing**: Where you buy things that become part of your products

> ➤ **Inventory levels**: What kind of stock you hold at different stages and locations of your manufacturing or distribution processes

> ➤ **Quality improvements**: What new features you have added to your product to address customer needs or expectations that have not been met

You are also likely to have a lot of data around parts replacement and warranties, which you probably use for part stocking and pricing types of decisions. Imagine if somebody could simulate your parts' usage data, maintenance of data on your equipment, and how your customers actually use your equipment. Precisely how you make money through maintenance programs and part sales is captured in this data. This data is not proprietary to you; your customers or their maintenance service contractors most likely own the data and somebody could just get it from them or buy it. They can now come up with very innovative maintenance programs for your equipment and take a substantial portion of your business away; you might be reduced to only a provider of proprietary parts.

As an illustration of a practical scenario for the preceding example, in large urban cities of emerging markets where potable water is a big issue, your company has decided to offer the base water purifier unit to households at a lesser margin, thereby trying to make the entry point attractive for customers. As a strategy, you recover your lost margin through replacements of purification candles, which frequently go bad. There is most likely nothing very proprietary or unique about the candle and changing those requires only basic technical skills. So, any small local entrepreneur can also take away your business, thus challenging your profits.

In both cases, you could be that "someone" if you understand the changing landscape stimulated by the power of big data.

To understand the changing landscape in the context of big data, there are six questions you need to consider:

> ➤ Do you know all the data you have?
> ➤ Do you understand all the data you have?
> ➤ Who else has similar data?
> ➤ What data are you using and how?
> ➤ How are others using similar data?
> ➤ What data from other sources do you use in your business?

By answering these questions, you should go beyond data that is easily captured; in fact, you should not even consider whether you capture these data elements today. Your compass in this exercise should be whether somebody or a system in your organization knows about these various data elements in any form—structured, unstructured, or streaming. These questions and the others that follow in this chapter might seem a bit tactical and low level compared to normal high-level strategic considerations, but because Big Data Analytics is so new, to be successful it is critical to build a solid foundation of understanding, with a lot of detail at a lower level to enable you to build the strategic framework. You need to avoid simply extrapolating general concepts and then basking in the luxury of making broad assumptions.

Once you have answered these questions, you need to compile the long list into an information catalog. Do not get distracted by the desire to classify the information elements into logical clusters at this point. Simply make the list and move on to the next step. In the following discussion, whenever we refer to information or data elements, we will consider all of what is available and what's possible, irrespective of ownership, collection, or storage.

Identifying the strategic implications

To understand strategic implications, you first need to understand the current role of data in your business. In order to help your understanding, you need to explore answers to four key questions:

> ➤ How many of the data elements are currently being used to influence your existing revenue and profit streams? Today, most of your considerations may be usual financial data related to P&L or balance sheet items.

> ➤ What is the contribution of your organization's data elements in the revenue and profit streams?

> ➤ What capabilities and business models do you have today to use the data?

> ➤ What capabilities and business models do you need to build or acquire to use the data?

Answers to these questions will lead you to areas that may be blind spots for your organization today in terms of both opportunities and threats. For example, in the previous example of the water purifier manufacturer, if you do not use maintenance records as a consideration in your revenue strategy, the implication is that you are possibly not exploiting a new maintenance model or replacement part sales opportunities, or even that somebody else might start doing it.

Let us consider another example. Anita has been banking with one particular bank for over 16 years and is extremely satisfied with their services. For all these years, she held salaried jobs and (thankfully) her salary grew several times. In addition to savings accounts, she has engaged in other types of transactions with this bank—all experiences were very satisfactory. However, recently she realized that this bank has handled less than 20 percent of her money. The bank did depute competent and nice managers to attract her business, and provided impeccable customer service to build credibility. They missed out on tracking her over the past 16 years across their various divisions to meet her needs of the hour. They had all her data, but used a quarterly savings account balance to pursue opportunities with her. This is another example of failing to understand strategic implications of data and analytics.

The problem is not the availability of data; it is appreciation of the value of data and what it can do for the business. Comprehending the strategic implications will lead you to conclusions that are not explicitly stated or obvious at a casual glance.

Spotting and simulating growing influences

Today, data is impacting your business more than you may realize. Before you go further into developing organizational strategies around big data, you need to understand the evolving influences of data and analytics on your business. You start this process by simulating the use of data by your organization in its current state, then understanding what your competitors are doing in this space, and finally understanding the correlation between different data points that impact your business.

Simulating your organization's use of data

You need to appreciate how the trajectory of your business has been influenced so far by the data elements you have used. You need to develop a historical perspective of this evolution process. For example, imagine you are a multi-purpose retailer such as a major grocery chain. Decades back, you would have used point-of-sale customer-buying data primarily to take an inventory and to make supply chain decisions. Over a period of time, you probably would have started using customer purchase data to understand affinities between items brought and how seasonality influences those decisions. Then, you most likely graduated to profiling customers on their social and economic background and understanding their buying behavior in those contexts. Today, you might even be using advanced customer analytics to proactively stock and push new or more items. You have graduated from using the same basic data to being more efficient and driving greater revenues and improving loyalty in a commoditized environment by giving a personalized experience to customers.

Understanding competitive actions

Next, you need to become familiar with how data-driven actions taken by others are influencing the course of your business and strategies. In the same continuing example, a start-up can use similar data obtained through cleverly designed surveys to become a recommendation channel and subsequently use this knowledge to drive collective bargains with you as a retailer, further challenging your current thin margins.

For this exercise, you need to scan competitors from your industry and all possible adjacencies to understand how they are using data to drive value in their business or even to change their business in terms of new ways of attracting revenue and customers, or possibly to make operations more profitable. The recommendation engine made extremely popular by Amazon is now replicated in many different industries.

Establishing correlations

Finally, to identify new possibilities, you need to gain new insights through the correlation of previously unpaired data elements. For example, as the large retailer being discussed, you have data on how much time your customers are spending in your store and how much they are spending in the snacks counter. Is there any correlation between the two? Assume that every customer who stays in your store for over two hours makes a purchase at the snacks counter. This creates additional business for you. If your snack counter is run by a franchisee, you can command higher rent by facilitating more traffic and purchases at the snack counter. You have found that 47 percent of your customers stay an average of 106 minutes per visit. Now that you know this, can you create incentives for your customers to stay for two hours or longer so that the likelihood of their visit to the snack counter increases? For example, you could engage your customers longer with a cooking show demonstration or a new product demonstration. With the right pairing of data and new insights derived from them, you can explore additional sources of revenue for your business.

Integrating new possibilities into planning

By following the steps in the preceding section, you will be able to identify "white spaces" in your business or "blue ocean markets." These lead to (hopefully many) new possibilities. You need to take them through a high level vetting process with your business leaders to ascertain the validity of pursuing them. The number of possibilities open to you is not necessarily important; it is more important that they have a high strategic impact for your business. The journey into big data can potentially bring obscure ideas to the forefront, which can seem very attractive at first glance. You need to consider everything and then make a move based on organizational appetite and competitive threats.

Tip

Novelty is difficult. It is rather challenging to integrate new possibilities into your strategic business planning. One effective technique for this effort is to transport your current world problems to a different world and solve the problem in the new world using data and technology. Then, bring back the solution to your current world and apply it. Following this, develop a plan to scale up the solution in your current world.

Developing strategies

Strategy is all about where to play and how to win. So far, we have discussed a bit about both. Different companies follow different processes and use different frameworks to develop their strategies. Companies adopt and adapt these approaches to meet their specific context and comfort. Big data analytics should never force you to abandon your current practices, but it should help augment them. There are two techniques that will assist you in this—gather as much data as possible and keep asking what kind of metrics or insights would you like to see out of the data. Let us look at some models.

The Balanced Score Card approach

Kaplan and Norton developed the renowned and much adopted **Strategy Map** and **Balanced Score Card** tools around the four seminal influences of **financial perspective, customer perspective, internal perspective,** and **learning and growth perspective**. While the Strategy Map translates and communicates the strategy for mass consumption, the Balanced Score Card approach provides the mechanism to cascade, deploy, and monitor the implementation of the strategy. These tools help executives educate the organization about the *value creation process* and its impact.

In creating the strategy map, Kaplan and Norton recommend keeping in mind the following different perspectives:

> ➤ **Financial Perspective**: This perspective is based on the creation of long-term shareholder value

> ➤ **Customer Perspective**: This perspective is based on clearly articulating the customer value proposition

> ➤ **Internal Perspective**: This perspective is based on improving processes around operations, customer management, innovation, regulatory, safety, community engagement, and other such areas

> ➤ **Learning and Growth Perspective**: This perspective is based on improving the talent pool, information systems, and organizational vigor

All of these considerations are already based on data; you can further strengthen the process by considering the complete spectrum. Let's reflect on a few examples:

You have an initiative around strategic pricing to improve your profitability. You are designing pricing strategies as part of this initiative around customer segmentation and the significance of your products and services to your customers. You will also look at some historical pricing data from your company, and may even stretch your research scope to the data from your competitors (if available) or get creative in exploring similar strategies adopted by non-adjacent suppliers to the same customer. To validate your theories, you will most likely run some experiments.

Now, how about you build a model that incorporates your customer's profitability, competitive pressures, market trends, and the share of your products and services into their revenue/profit delivery cycles? Most of this data is available today and may not be easy to access or analyze. This will most likely be a combination of unstructured and streaming data. But if you can build a comprehensive model that big data analytics can enable you to do, you can have a very robust pricing strategy that will significantly benefit your business. If your company makes an 8 percent return on sales, then a 1 percent pricing improvement leads to a 12.5 percent improvement on your current shareholder returns.

Let's consider another example from a different domain:

In most organizations, the HR department maintains an inventory of skills its employees possess. The supervisors of the employees will usually validate those skills; sometimes tests are conducted to assess the skill levels. Most of the skills that are recorded are oriented towards what what employees need to do their job. Employees are learning new skills, getting new experiences, and possibly have expertise in non-job related fields, which might be of use for the company. These snippets of information will usually not be stored in a traditional skill inventory system; definitely not on anywhere close to a real-time basis. However, if we leverage the social media aspects of a company and the data captured through in-process activities, we will get insights into the new nuggets of information just described. So now you can enrich your traditional skill inventory with new learning enabled by big data.

Therefore, while developing strategies, there are two major questions you need to keep in mind:

➤ Have you considered all the possible data?
➤ Does your improved understanding of all data bring any new possibilities?

Regardless of which strategy framework you currently use, these questions are universally useful.

Force Field Analysis

Force Field Analysis is another technique many strategy experts use. This can be a very practical and easy method, especially when applied to create a growth roadmap using big data.

In Force Field Analysis, you have essentially two states and two forces:

➤ The two states are:

    ➢ **Current state:** This represents the current state of your business in terms of market position, profitability, revenue, or any other parameter on which you want to do a comparison

    ➢ **Future state:** This represents the future desired state of your business on the same terms of comparison as current state analysis

➤ The two forces are:

    ➢ **Enabling forces:** These are the driving forces that help you achieve your goals of moving from current to future state

    ➢ **Restraining forces:** These are the limiting forces that resist your efforts to achieve your desired future state

We start Force Field Analysis by drawing two parallel lines that represent a current state and desired state going from left to right to show progression. Then, we include all the enabling forces on the left-hand side of the current state. Then we put all the restraining forces to the right of the current state line. To make it more interesting, you can actually change the length and thickness of the arrows that represent the various forces relative to their impact on enabling or restraining. This form of representation allows us to visually understand at a glance what factors are at play to further or slow down our strategy. This is a good starting point to identify strategic initiatives that will enable us to overcome the challenges.

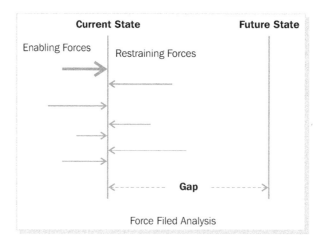

Force Filed Analysis

Please remember that you may not always be able to eliminate all the restraining forces. Once you have the preceding diagram for your business, you need to work on making some of the enabling forces more potent and try reducing the potency of some of the restraining forces so that you are able to reduce the net gap.

If you replace *forces* with *data* in the preceding diagram, and apply the same action decision principles, you can draw a roadmap of how to use data from your existing data repository to reach your desired state of business.

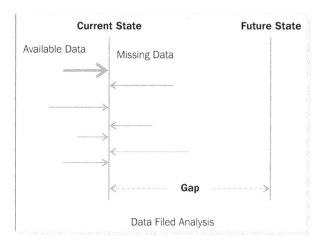

Aligning existing initiatives

Aligning existing big data analytics initiatives in organizations is extremely critical. Parallel initiatives draw upon a lot of valuable organizational resources, creating stress for other projects. Moreover, executives and shareholders can sometimes get disillusioned and confused by the plethora of initiatives trying to do somewhat similar things, and in the process can become unsure about whether the initiatives will deliver the desired results. At an extreme, they might even consider big data analytics as yet another fad and wait for it to play out before taking any decisive action.

There is no magic bullet that can solve this problem. Every company is trying to figure things out in a manner suitable to their context and culture. If there are many initiatives running in your organization, it is a good thing—there are more people who are exposed to the power of big data and they are trying to solve many business problems using these capabilities. If they begin to collaborate, they can all learn from each other in using the technology and analytics better. They can also benefit from the new insights that interplay between the various initiatives present. This way, you may be able to reach answers to your business problems faster.

It is also critical to get some insights from data and analytics sooner rather than later. This helps to win the confidence of executives in the program; it also helps to continuously refine the results and insights.

You can take a very disciplined and collaborative approach towards aligning various big data initiatives in your company:

➤ Make a list of all initiatives in the company that use data as the primary tool for a business outcome. These initiatives may not necessarily bear the big data tag, but you need to qualify whether the projects are using at least a high volume or high velocity or high variety data in its quest.

➤ Identify the strategic intent of these projects. Find out what business outcome these initiatives are trying to influence.

➤ Understand what is common and what is different between the approaches and outcomes of the different initiatives.

➤ Classify initiatives into similar clusters of strategic intents of business outcomes.

➤ Investigate whether the efforts of one initiative in a cluster can improve the performance of another initiative.

➤ Differentiate activities around solving infrastructure issues and delivering user outcomes. The differences will usually manifest themselves in the different approaches. This step allows you to take another pass at spotting the differences and commonalities.

➤ Find out how much investment each initiative is going to require and how long they are expected to last. You need to answer this question in the context of infrastructure development and outcome delivery.

➤ Prioritize different initiatives, first based on expected benefits, then on required time, and finally on the basis of planned investments.

➤ Create a map for most optimal initiatives geared towards achieving the strategic intent of the organization.

➤ Secure executive buy-in for your strategic roadmap of the collated initiatives. When competing groups reach out to the executive team for their sponsorship, they need to support your roadmap and point of view.

➤ Communicate your detailed research and the resulting map to the project teams. This will help them understand your strategic intent and align their interests and efforts towards broader and more impactful organizational goals.

➤ Reallocate resources and investments based on this alignment. Establish a robust and fair governance process around the investments. We will talk more about this topic in Chapter 6, Managing the Money: Investment, Monetization and Performance Management when we talk about investments and financial management.

➤ Review the entire process every six months at the latest. People will find new use cases for big data. Technical and financial barriers for pursuing such use cases are low. The proliferation of further initiatives is unavoidable and undesirable, so aligning them quickly is beneficial for your organization.

All the existing projects in your organization have most likely been initiated by some motivated individuals who see value in applying Big Data Analytics to solve business problems. In many cases, such projects may not have executive sponsorship and the project leader and team members are pursuing these as their labor of love to prove something new to the broader organization. Big data is often known to bring out entrepreneurial traits in people. Remember, people's passion and pain is associated with each of these projects. We do not want to discourage such behavior, but our objective is to channel their efforts and energies. The alignment exercise needs to be handled with care and compassion. We want the big data ecosystem in the company not only viable and valuable, but also vibrant.

Cascading your strategy

After you have developed your strategy and harmonized all existing initiatives around it, now you need to communicate the strategy to the rest of the organization. You want the various teams in your business to align with that strategy and build their plans, goals, and execution capabilities around it. This process is called strategic cascade. It is about more than simple communication. A strategy cascade involves breaking down the strategy into context relevant for the various teams and developing their business plan and monitoring mechanisms around it.

A good strategic cascade will go into some detail and should be done for each of the individual initiatives that are triggered by the various strategies. To effectively cascade your big data strategies, you need to compose, clarify, and communicate your strategy framework to the entire organization in the context of data and its implications. Big data is pervasive and the strategy you develop and implement will have a bearing on everybody in the company. Big data is also for everybody; whether your company is big or small, you could equally benefit from big data. You need to translate the different facets of your big data strategy and the resulting initiatives into something that the entire organization will understand. Big data is an evolving discipline. The more people you can get on board your big data journey, the more hands you have to exploit the new emerging capabilities. You will also have a bigger pool of people who can see new value in data and create new value from data. Lofty and vague explanations can be confusing and interpreted differently. While designing your cascade plans, it is crucial to specify micro level details so that people understand clearly and nothing is left to speculation.

A normal strategic cascade follows a systematic process. The following diagram is a representation used when developing the cascade, and many organizations use formats similar to this:

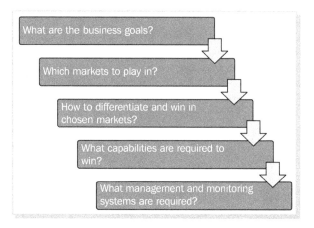

Let's consider an example of how to develop a strategy cascade. Imagine you are a manufacturer of capital intensive equipment that is used by generic hospital and schools—say X-ray machines. In most cases, you have maintenance contracts with your customers. As part of these contracts, you are responsible for the general upkeep of your equipment and provide replacement parts at discounted rates. After careful and detailed studies, you have arrived at the conclusion that using Big Data Analytics, you can significantly grow your service business, which gives you good profits and also helps you secure repeat business. Let's now develop a strategy cascade using the methodology outlined in the preceding figure:

➤ What are the business goals?

  ➤ Increase service revenue by 30 percent in 3 years

➤ Which markets can we play in?

  ➤ K-12 schools market in tier-1 and tier-2 cities

The reason for selecting this market is that in such locations, customers have limited choices and they are difficult for your traditional competitors to cover. In each school, you may only have 1 machine. However, when you add up all the schools in a state you are now talking very big numbers. Such machines are also sold to hospitals at a good profit margin. However, as part of your strategy you choose to ignore the more seemingly profitable hospital segment for this initiative because you have found they have more internal capabilities to service your equipment and are less reliant on you other than for parts.

  ➤ How to differentiate between and win in the chosen markets?

  ➤ Provide predictive analytics on how to increase the equipment life and reduce operating costs, and offer other advisory services around student health by enabling a larger community of health experts from around the nation.

The reason you choose this differentiation approach is that your small time local entrepreneurs who can provide regular routine inspection and maintenance services will find it difficult to extend their offering portfolio.

- ➤ What capabilities are required to win?
    - ➢ Remotely connecting to equipment very inexpensively
    - ➢ Store and analyze the performance data that comes from those X-ray machines (not the X-rays themselves as privacy issues may be involved)
    - ➢ Service team or channel that can respond to the needs of customers
    - ➢ A team of statisticians, engineers, and other experts who can continuously keep doing more experimental analysis
    - ➢ A team of expert doctors who can be made available using technology to help your schools
- ➤ What management and monitoring systems are required?
    - ➢ New business models, operating disciplines, and monitoring and review mechanisms to ensure business goals are met

Many of these steps may seem similar to traditional IT initiatives; however, when we take into account the huge volumes and variety of data, and consider both structured and unstructured data, this initiative becomes a big data problem.

The simplified strategy cascade for the preceding situation can be represented in the following manner.

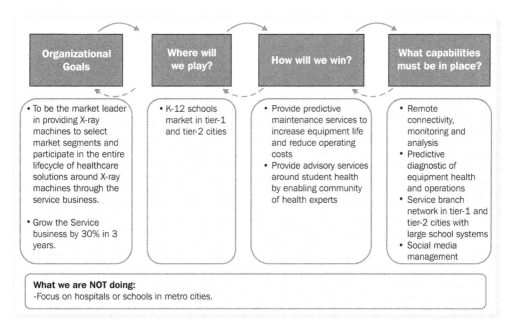

The above format is a tool that you can use to communicate and cascade your strategy to the rest of the business. If you choose a different format, make sure it is visual and easy to follow. Once you have developed your strategy cascade, it is clear to your team and the rest of the organization which markets are you vying for, how you plan to differentiate your business to win more in those markets, what kind of tools and capabilities you need to differentiate and win, and how you are going to monitor and manage the initiatives around growth. Your team and the rest of the business are now aligned with your plans and all geared up to go and win.

Summary

In this chapter, we worked on several topics that will help you move ahead in your journey of big data analytics:

- We discussed the strategic implications put forward by big data analytics
- We built a Business Catalog that lists various sources of revenue for your business and key areas of operations
- We identified how big data analytics is influencing our business and how those influences grow over a period of time
- We developed an Information Catalog for your business
- We worked on integrating the new possibilities brought forward by big data analytics into our business
- We developed organizational strategies around big data analytics
- We aligned various existing big data analytics initiatives to drive better synergies and achieve exponential results
- Finally, we created a framework on how to cascade the strategic value and intent of big data analytics across your organization

You are now armed with the power to understand what big data analytics can do for your business, and where and how it can help you win in the market place. Use big data analytics as part of your strategy to make things happen.

Browsing the net, quite some time back, I came across a very profound quote whose author is anonymous:

> *"There are three kinds of companies, those that make things happen, those that watch things happen, and those that wonder what happened."*

In the next chapter, we will work on building an opportunity landscape for your business enabled by the capabilities of big data analytics. In doing so, we will work on how to take a structured approach in identifying and keep adding to your opportunity portfolio.

2

Creating an Opportunity Landscape and Collecting Your Gold Coins

In the previous chapter, we worked on identifying parts of your business where we can unlock untapped value by applying big data analytics and integrating its possibilities into your strategic framework. Now, let's work on identifying what specific opportunities to pursue. Big data should not be seen as panacea for all organizational pursuits. There are certain scenarios where big data capabilities can help organizations understand problems or opportunities and make decisions. In this chapter, we will work on identifying these scenarios. Happy hunting!

Let's first review the major changes that are enabled by big data. In their distinguished book *Big Data: A Revolution That Will Transform How We Live, Work and Think*, Prof. Viktor Mayer-Schonberger and Mr. Kenneth Cukier talk about 3 major changes:

➤ The ability to process all or vast amounts of data. This is important because now you are no longer limited by sample sizes and surface assumptions.

➤ The ability to accept a variety and disorderliness of data. This helps you use large quantities of data irrespective of the source and quality of data.

➤ The ability to create hypotheses around what is going to happen without deeply understanding why it happens. This is especially important because now the pressure to identify causality becomes less critical since large volumes of data lead to likely pattern repetitions.

Make a note

I found that this book was a very good starting point to use when learning about the evolution, applications, and future of big data. I recommend readers to consider reviewing this book as well: http://www.amazon.com/Big-Data-Revolution-Transform-Think/dp/0544002695.

Clearly, big data extends your capabilities, opening up new possibilities that can really help your business.

However, a note of caution is required here. In most cases, big data projects start with analyzing smaller sample sizes of data before the analytics is run on terabytes of data. Using sample data was the only option earlier to reach a conclusion since massive data processing was so complex and expensive. Now you are not constrained by what data and how much data can you store and process, you will most likely run several analyses on different sample data and then test your hypotheses on significantly larger volumes of data. If you are dealing with largely erroneous or bad data, your conclusions will mirror the quality of data. Big data will not make bad data better; it will simply help identify it and get around them. Even though you may not have to worry about causality much, it will be helpful to understand the sources of data to understand the context of the data.

Companies often plunge straight into a big data initiative after being inspired by the possibilities. Sometimes inspiration comes because of a new executive joining, or some senior management staff attending some workshops on the topic, or because of a successful pitch made by consulting companies. Regardless of where inspiration comes from, your organization needs to take a very structured and systematic approach to identifying the macro landscape of opportunities.

Building your Data Catalog

In *Chapter 1, Building Your Strategy Framework*, we worked on building a Business Catalog and a related Information Catalog. These are your starting points to build your **Data Catalog**. For each of the identified revenue sources or business or operations areas, you already have a list of various information topics that you currently have or can get access to. Now for each of these information topics, you need to list the detailed data elements, including both *what you have* and *what you need* to fully understand the topic and generate value from it. For doing this exercise, you will need help from your IT experts who are responsible for the maintenance of data-related systems, as well as from users of those systems who actually understand the data can provide some kind of context for it. Sometimes it is good to get the viewpoint of employees who are not connected to the different IT systems, but have a deep understanding of the business in terms of what information and data it runs on.

Building this Data Catalog will help you get a perspective on data usage and how it impacts your business. This perspective will help you identify prospects for using data more effectively or in different ways to drive the growth and sustainability of your business.

The Gold Coin approach

Gold Coin is a contained project that leverages the power of advanced analytics to create tangible value from data that may not have been tapped previously. A Gold Coin is usually an easily manageable sized project that has small but measurable value that grows over a period of time. The growth in economic value of a Gold Coin happens because of the higher appreciation of the benefits of the outcome from the project and/or greater adoption across your business. I was first introduced to the concept of Gold Coins by Mr. Howard is currently Senior Vice President of Innovation and Development at Allstate Insurance in US. Howard has spent decades in his career across various companies and industries identifying these small nuggets of value from data and analytics while striving for the larger benefits.

Gold Coins are a great way to rally organizational excitement and energy for a broader pursuit of data and analytics programs. There are a number of reasons for this:

> ➤ The scope of a Gold Coin project is typically limited to a particular business area or part of the organization. The scope and outcome expected from the project is normally quite well defined. The uncomplicated boundary of a Gold Coin project simplifies it for people to absorb the intent, content, and attempt the project themselves.

> ➤ Since a Gold Coin project is largely enclosed in one part of the current business, to pursue the project, the team working on it or even the larger organization does not have to go through lot of new learning about the business process. The limited scope, less required resources, and defined timeline ensures higher success in the uncharted waters of Big Data Analytics.

> ➤ A Gold Coin project works on existing data that could not be previously harnessed due to technology challenges. A Gold Coin project does not require stretching current understanding of the business; it only exposes new possibilities. So, the appeal to the project team and organization beyond is straightforward.

> ➤ A Gold Coin project ends up demonstrating tangible economic benefits through new insights, new offerings, and modified operational processes. These are easy to compare with similar parts of the business where the current project is occurring. So, repeating the project and replicating the benefits is relatively easy. They are easy to vault.

To summarize, Gold Coins are:

> ➤ Easy to understand
> ➤ Easy to manage
> ➤ Easy to communicate
> ➤ Easy to commercialize

Identifying your Gold Coins

In developing your strategy framework to exploit big data in your business, you did a couple of things that will help you identify Gold Coins—you created an Information Catalog and identified white spaces (portions of your existing market place that you have not addressed so far) or blue ocean markets (new markets that are still untapped by you or any other competitor) that you want to tackle. Earlier in this chapter, you took those as a base and developed your Data Catalog. Your Data Catalog should help you identify the way you currently use information and how insights help to drive your current business practices. Your goal is not to create a data library with very clear definitions and relationships that are required by a database analyst or programmer to develop an application to meet your business goals; we have not reached that stage yet! To start your Gold Coin identification, as long as you have easily understandable business definitions of information and insight, you are good to go.

You first need to take a particular aspect of your business—specific revenue streams or departments. You then need to understand the Data Catalog in greater detail—what is available, what is being used, how the data is being used to drive decisions, how value is created for customers, and how value is being created for your business. Next, you then find out whether there is data in the catalog that cannot be currently leveraged due to limitations of your technology infrastructure. For example, you have a lot of unstructured data from disparate sources, but are not able to create a set of common insights about a topic using such data. A practical scenario for this example could be customer feedback received from paper-based surveys, feedback into a web portal, or customer feedback received through e-mails. You have the data, and you also have a lot of valuable insight in this feedback data, but you may not have the means to make sense of the information contained in different systems, different formats, and captured differently. In another example, you may have lot of structured streaming data such as web clicks by visitors on your web portal, but cannot store and analyze it effectively and in real time.

Make a note

If you can somehow unlock the unused data into new insights that can possibly lead to new offerings or new operational processes, you have identified a Gold Coin idea.

To qualify a Gold Coin idea, you can follow a simple three step process:

1. Qualification.
2. Benefit assessment.
3. Strategic advantage assessment.

Qualification

There are six qualifiers that help define big data:

➤ **Volume**: You have lots of data, usually running into terabytes and petabytes

➤ **Velocity**: Either your organization is creating data at a very fast pace, say lot of data every minute or more frequently, or your organization may be the recipient of a lot of data every few seconds or minutes

➤ **Variety**: You have data from different sources and in different formats that all look very different

➤ **Veracity**: You have fidelity or reliability issues with the data because of how it is generated and collected

➤ **Visualization**: You need the ability to represent the complexity of data and the insights derived from it in a manner easy for business users and executives to act upon

➤ **Viability**: You need to use the volume, and variety of data in a flexible way on a long-term sustainable basis

You need to consider whether at least two factors from the list of big data qualifiers are applicable.

In the X-ray machine example we discussed in *Chapter 1, Building Your Strategy Framework*, for the new service business, the company will have to capture high *volume* and high *velocity* data. Since there are manual service records in consideration, there is also a good deal of *variety*. Variety is further accentuated because you are also building an interaction portal for medical experts who will have very differently formatted and structured streaming data. Due to communication link failures, there may be trust-related issues with the data, so there is veracity in play as well.

Benefit assessment

You must be able to articulate at least one tangible benefit and one intangible customer-centric benefit that will come out of pursuing this project. Without a full blown development of the idea, try using the data and apply some basic desk research analysis to see whether your assumptions about the benefits are likely to hold ground with the sample test results.

In the preceding example, new service revenues are a clear and tangible business benefit. You are also offering your customers—the schools, the nurses, the students, and the teachers—access to the medical expert's portal. Through this, they will get expert advice. Since you are the one making it available, your customers will look up to you as providing additional value beyond your normal scope of work. You will be viewed differently than other manufacturers and maintenance service providers. This will help promote better relationship with your customers. When you are trying to renew your contract or get additional business, this relationship will help you. This is a great intangible benefit in this example.

Strategic advantage assessment

Finally, the benefits identified must provide your business with a strategic advantage—they must differentiate your business or operations and must help you secure more business or improve profits. They should also provide an advantage to your business ahead of the competition. Sometimes you will find that another company, a competitor, or an adjacent player is using data and analytics to disrupt your business. In such cases, you might have to use a Gold Coins idea to respond to competitive threats.

Gold Coin examples

Now, we will look at some examples of Gold Coins. These examples may be from an industry different than yours; they are for illustrative purpose to show you how to go about identifying Gold Coins.

Problem 1 – service parts historical analysis

Your company is in the business of providing technical maintenance services for its highly engineered and custom built electro-mechanical products. Your company has been in business for a very long time and operates globally today. The technical maintenance services are managed locally through a branch network and some select channel partners with whom your company has long-standing relationships. The service technicians record their maintenance activities in service reports that are filed with your company. Careful reviews of past maintenance service records reveals a lot about the issues customers have faced with your equipment, possibly how they used your products, and what parts and consumables they brought from you or others.

Decades back, all such service records used to be maintained in hard paper copies and archived in storage facilities. Over the years, some level of automation has been introduced into this business area. However, the level of automation varies from location to location. It has also been progressively evolving; this means that certain data around maintenance records are manually stored in certain years, but exist in a structured database in following years.

Your company also has records either manual or digital around all parts purchased by different customers and channel partners. But these parts purchase records are not always tied directly to the products your company has manufactured and sold.

If you are able to understand the parts consumption pattern based on history, usage, and age of the equipment that it is part of, and if you're able to find out affinities between what parts are usually purchased together, it can create new opportunities around proactive part sales, strategic pricing for higher margins, and creating kits of related parts.

Can this be a Gold Coin?

Problem 2 – customer records aggregation

Your company operates across multiple customer segments and geographies in a business to business (B2B) environment. Your company sells its products and services through various channels. You collect many different types of customer information at various stages of engagement with your customers throughout the life cycle of your products and services. However, there is no single view of customers across different product lines or geographies or types of services offered. Some of the customer-related data is stored in structured databases in your company's IT systems, and the rest exists in all types of unstructured or physical (paper-based) repositories.

The lack of a common view between customers and customer data limits your company's ability to explore more opportunities around cross-selling and up-selling. It also limits your company's ability to understand customer needs for future product/service development initiatives.

Is this a Gold Coin?

Problem 3 – mining corporate social media to understand employee engagement

Employee engagement is a key priority for your company. Your company genuinely believes that employees are a strategic differentiator for your business. Your management team undertakes many efforts such as periodic surveys, town hall meetings, and other forms of interactions to gauge employee engagement with the company.

Recently, your company has been promoting collaboration between employees through deployment of technology. Now there are a number of platforms that offer Facebook-type features for employees to interact with each other, form online communities, share knowledge, store information and documents, and work on projects together. Your company has implemented one such platform and has adopted rather liberal policies to promote social collaboration. The primary areas of implementation for this platform are sales and engineering, but access has been given across many departments. Your employees have reciprocated this with heavy usage of the corporate social media platform; adoption is quite extensive across divisions, branches, and demographic groups with younger employees leading the charge.

Employees are using the social media platform to also express their opinions about various products and policies of the company. Every day, many times within the day, employees share their opinion. The feedback does not necessarily follow any structure and one can manually go through all the posts to gauge the mood of employees. Technology can solve this problem and allow you to get to the insights faster; it can help the company react more meaningfully and in a timely manner to employee feedback.

Is this a Gold Coin?

Gold Coins are in plain sight all over your business. You may not have considered these opportunities due to other priorities or technical limitations, many of which big data is solving for you. Now that you have seen how simple everyday activities and problems can lead to you identifying Gold Coins, start making a list. In the next section, we shall assess them and then prioritize them.

Assessing your Gold Coin project

Next you need to develop a simple assessment framework. First, you should start with the key objective or expected outcome from the Gold Coin idea and then answer the following questions:

> ➤ Do we need to process millions of records or terabytes of data to achieve the project objectives? (Volume)

> ➤ Do we have data coming constantly at very frequent intervals, say less than every 15 minutes? (Velocity)

> ➤ Do we have data from multiple sources that have some common elements but look very different and are not easy to normalize? (Variety)

> ➤ Are there intermittent trust issues with some of the data that come in? (Veracity)

> ➤ Is there a dire need to get creative with visually representing the data for business users and customers to understand intuitively? (Visualization)

> ➤ Will we be able to get such data in future if we want to repeat this project for this part of the business and other similar parts of the business? (Viability)

> ➤ Do we have tangible benefits for our business? (Tangible benefits)

> ➤ Is this project going to make our products/services more useful for our customers? (Customer benefits)

> ➤ Does this project give us any competitive advantage? (Competitive advantage)

If you answer yes twice or more between questions one and four and answer yes to the remainder of the questions, your Gold Coin idea is a valid Gold Coin project worth pursuing using big data. If you satisfy only one of the first four criteria and none from the rest, there might be choices other than the big data approach to reach your goals.

Now let us explore the preceding examples in the context of the assessment criteria:

Criteria	Problem 1 **Service Parts Historical Analysis**	Problem 2 **Customer Records Mash-up**	Problem 3 **Social Media Data and Employee Engagement**
Volume	Yes	Yes	Yes
Velocity	Yes	No	Yes
Variety	Yes	Yes	Yes
Veracity	Yes	Yes	Yes
Visualization	Yes	Yes	No
Viability	Yes	Yes	Yes
Tangible benefits	Yes	Yes	No
Customer benefits	Yes	Yes	Yes
Competitive advantage	Yes	Yes	Yes

From the preceding assessment, it is clear that *Service Parts Historical Analysis* and *Customer Records Mash-up* qualify as Gold Coin projects. While the analysis of corporate social media data to understand employee engagement is a valid big data problem in the domain of human resources, it need not necessarily be pursued as a Gold Coin project because it does not create direct tangible benefits and it does not require sophisticated visualization of the data—only textual insights from a simple demographic analysis is adequate.
There will always be situations where you need to make a judgment call along with your management team or key staff members about whether you should pursue a particular problem as a Gold Coin project.

Prioritizing your Gold Coins

The universal appeal of Gold Coin projects make it very attractive for people. Before you realize, your business will be blossoming with Gold Coin ideas. Since they are inherently self-funding in nature, the usual roadblocks of getting them approved and started will not be an impediment. You will end up spending considerable time assessing and qualifying such Gold Coin projects and any time remaining in managing them. In such circumstances, it is critical that you prioritize your Gold Coins.

There are many factors on which you can evaluate your Gold Coin ideas:

> **New revenue sources**: Does this Gold Coin give you any ideas for pursuing new sources of profitable revenue? In the example given in Problem 1 in the earlier section with examples of Gold Coins, you can create new part kit options that attract higher revenues and margins. The concept of combo meals offered by many fast food joints is an example similar to this. So, pursuing this Gold Coin takes a higher priority compared to the employee engagement data that generates a lot of valuable insights but does not necessarily create any new revenue ideas.

> **Competitive advantage**: Does this Gold Coin give you an edge over your competitors and is it difficult for them to replicate? In the example of the customer records mash-up, if your competitors suffer from similar challenges around data harmony and roll-up, and if they do not have structured big data initiatives like you do, it will give you an edge in understanding your customers better. The early lead will force your competitors to adopt defensive strategies that are less effective and more expensive. Google established a market leadership (enough to be considered a monopoly maybe) in online adverts through a very similar strategy.

> **Tangible value to business**: Even if your Gold Coin project does not lead to any direct revenue source or does not give you a clear competitive advantage, does it create tangible value for your business that contributes to the organization's bottom-line? For many organizations that have a legacy of unstructured data, data normalization is a herculean task and can be a traumatic experience for those involved. Using **Natural Language Processing** and **Bayesian Networks**, many big data capabilities make data normalization almost effortless. This helps unlock the untapped value of data in those disparate sources.

Make a note

Google Research has done a lot of good work in this space and most of their findings are available on their website. You can find more information on that by visiting `http://research.google.com/pubs`.

Carnegie Mellon University has also done extensive research in this space and offer tailored courses to help people become proficient in these topics. You can find more information on this by visiting `http://www.cs.cmu.edu/~nasmith/nlp-cl.html`.

> **Value appreciation**: Gold Coins appreciate over time. Some of them will have greater value as time goes by because you will have more data leading to newer insights and newer opportunities. Some of them will have a lot of benefit and impact now, but the data that they are based on might lose its relevance over a period of time. In the earlier section, we were looking at two examples—one where we are analyzing how your parts business is working and another where you are aggregating your customer records (Problems 1 and 2). In the former, the analysis and insights are less likely to change over time if the parent equipment or its usage does not change much, so it will have limited value appreciation once you solve the original problem.

For the later example, when you know more things about your customers and what triggers them to buy something, your insights into customers' buying patterns will improve. So if you have to choose only one project, choose this one, helping you make sense of different data about customers and their buying behavior, should get priority, because over a period of time the new insights will lead you to new revenue opportunities and/or more profitable business models. However, be sure to check with your business leaders and sponsors what they consider as immediate priorities.

➤ **Data availability**: Finally, the availability of data in any form plays a key role in prioritizing your Gold Coin projects. To pursue every new Gold Coin idea, you need data to perform analytics. If getting this data becomes very difficult and expensive, such projects take a lower priority. For example, the parts history analysis example is a powerful Gold Coin idea, but if your company does not store any parts usage and history information, there is no point in pursuing this idea at this point until you put in the infrastructure to first collect the data.

Developing the prioritization framework

The way you created a formal assessment framework, you should also create a formal prioritization framework where all projects are evaluated objectively. This is important because it will help you communicate to the various stakeholders and also your project team on your decision making process. As we discussed earlier, your team and your stakeholders need to be fully engaged and included in the process.

The following table is an example of a prioritization framework:

Criteria	Threshold Values	Project1	Project2	Project3
New revenue impact	High: >1 million dollars Medium: >250K dollars s<1 million dollars Low: < 250K dollars			
Competitive advantage	High: unique in industry Medium: difficult to copy Low: defensive strategy			

Criteria	Threshold Values	Project1	Project2	Project3
Business impact (margin impact in this example)	High: > 50 basis points (bps) Medium: > 10 <50 bps Low: <10 bps			
Value appreciation	High: 3x in 3 years Medium: 2x in 3 years Low: <2x in 3 years			
Data availability	High: >90 percent available Medium: >70 percent available Low: <70 percent available			

Depending on the specific nature and situation of your business, you can determine threshold values, but you need to arrive at standard tiered values so that you can have a near equitable comparison. The values in the preceding framework are only illustrative in nature.

Once you decide on the thresholds and apply the framework, score each project and rank them before you validate it with your executive leadership or project sponsors. Please remember that *at this point, you are working with indicative values.* So please do not spend too much time defending or analyzing any specific value. But be sure to prepare your executive leadership and project sponsors that you are working on indicative values that might change after further work in the project and thereby you may be required to reprioritize (with their consent and knowledge) later based on new learning.

All Gold Coins are not equal. There are bound to be many esoteric ideas that people will encourage you passionately to pursue and they might have a strong reasoning why those ideas need to be taken up. You will always be limited by resources—time, money, and expertise. You need to take the best possible decision on which Gold Coin is worth your attention and perusal.

Building your Gold Mine

Now you have started collecting your Gold Coins and building your opportunity landscape with Big Data. You have begun the exciting journey of building a large and very valuable portfolio of Gold Coins into a Gold Mine that will create unparalleled shareholder value for your business.

The possibilities are exhilarating; you will soon find it difficult to keep up pace with the flurry of Gold Coins and all the excitement around them. You need to take a very structured approach to keep looking for new Gold Coins and building the Gold Mine for your business. This will stop you from getting swamped and losing organizational momentum with your big data project. You have already worked on many tools that will help you in this hunt for Gold Coins.

In the previous chapter, you built a Business Catalog and an Information Catalog. In this you started with building a Data Catalog. Now, you'll build an Opportunity Catalog. Your Opportunity Catalog is a simple listing of all the possible Gold Coins along in the context of your Business Catalog and Information Catalog. Your Opportunity Catalog also contains the benefits or business value and ranking/prioritization of all your Gold Coins. The following table gives you a simple illustration of what the Opportunity Catalog could look like for you. You should adapt it to what suits your needs and organizational practices. For the purpose of this exercise, we will use the same examples of Gold Coin projects discussed earlier in this chapter.

Business Catalog	Information Catalog	Gold Coin Project	Business Value	Priority
Maintenance Services	Service history	Part kitting and campaign design		
Maintenance Services	Service history	Optimal parts stocking decisions		
Customer Information	Customer data and sales and service data	Customer records mash-up for new cross-sell up-sell opportunities		
Human Resources	Employee feedback	Employee engagement monitoring		

It is good to get started with whatever you can lay your hands on easily and where your management/executive leadership sees value. However, you need to list all the possible revenue streams and operations area to build your Business Catalog; all the possible information areas present in those keep identifying more and more Gold Coin ideas.

The best place to start is either in sections of your business where you are making lot of money or bleeding lot of money to competitors or internal operational gaps. Being able to show some concrete financial benefits in a short span of time always helps the interest and momentum of such initiatives. It also helps in creating the infrastructure to explore future Gold Coins and build your big data analytics organizational platform.

We recommend that every quarter, you get together a cross-functional team with various departments of your business represented, and review your Gold Coin Opportunity Catalog. In this forum, you should include people from different organizational hierarchies because they present very different perspectives about where opportunities lie. However, do not limit this only to your company's executive leadership or working field people. This group can become your guiding coalition for the big data initiative in your organization; they can be your primary evangelists as well. This process also helps spread the positive momentum around big data analytics initiatives in your organization.

You should build a structured project plan. There are many types of software—both paid and open source—that you can use for project planning and tracking. **Microsoft Project** is a good tool that has been around for a long time. If you do not have access to any tools or do not have the patience for using them, use spreadsheets. The key is to build one project plan and track it. This will help you monitor progress and communicate the same to your stakeholders. We recommend you also build a physical chart or mock-up model of a Gold Mine and keep filling them with gold coin shaped bits of paper, each representing a Gold Coin project. In our experience, we have found these physical manifestations of conceptual quests very useful as they help people to visually understand the progress. As time goes by, it also is a good reminder for you that your hard work is helping further your organization's growth.

Summary

In this chapter, you developed some perceptible opportunities around big data from some concepts and strategies discussed in the previous chapter. By now, you have:

➤ Built a Data Catalog

➤ Understood the concept of crafting business opportunities using big data analytics into Gold Coin projects

➤ Identified your Gold Coins

➤ Assessed and prioritized your Gold Coins

➤ Created your Opportunity Catalog and started building your Gold Mine

You are now all set to get started and raring to go.

You can get started even if you have one Gold Coin. If you are part of a smaller organization, a start-up, or just getting initiated into big data, starting with one Gold Coin is a good idea. If you have more, select the top highest ranked ones and build project teams and plans around those. It is better not to start too many because there is valuable learning from each of the projects that will help you refine your future course of action. Initially, each Gold Coin project will need lot of time from you; you will also in parallel need to work on building the future big data analytics roadmap and platform for your business. So it is essential that you keep the scope and portfolio to a point that you can manage it easily. You need to design the Gold Coin projects in a way that you can see an evident value in ideally three months. In today's connected world with information overflow and ever squeezing market forces, a short turnaround of benefits is always appreciated by executive leadership and shareholders.

In the next chapter, we will work on how to develop and implement an effective project management methodology to realize these Gold Coins. We will take some unique approaches to managing the differently complex big data analytics initiatives.

3

Managing Your Big Data Projects Effectively

To realize the full potential of Big Data, companies need to pursue several parallel initiatives, as follows:

> ➤ Create a strong pool of qualified resources to drive various initiatives
> ➤ Build momentum around the adoption of Big Data technologies
> ➤ Build critical mass of success in Big Data projects
> ➤ Build a long-term, robust, and sustainable platform for Big Data initiatives

There are many established methodologies followed in traditional technology-driven projects. At one end of the spectrum, we have the classical waterfall model, which takes a very sequential view of projects from start to finish for the entire scope of the project. At the other end of the spectrum, we have the new-age agile methodologies, which promote a more iterative approach addressing smaller chunks of the scope at a time. The project management techniques for all of them are quite mature; there is a wealth of information in published literature, case studies, and training and certification programs. Big Data projects, however, need to be managed differently. Innovative approaches are necessary to effectively address the novelty and unique nature of Big Data.

In the previous chapters, we worked on identifying in which parts of your business we can develop new value-creation opportunities using Big Data and how we can go about the identification process using the Gold Coin approach. For the identified value to be realized, the linked projects have to be managed and executed effectively. If you are part of an organization that is just starting on a Big Data journey or has had limited success in the past, this chapter will help you develop project-management techniques that will increase the probability of your success.

Recognizing how Big Data Analytics projects are different

In Chapter 2, Creating an Opportunity Landscape and Collecting Your Gold Coins, we discussed the three major changes caused by Big Data Analytics—the ability to process all data and the ability to manage data disorderliness and allow correlation to trump causality. These fundamental shifts radically transform our ability to leverage technology. There are a number of differences between traditional technology projects and Big Data projects. Let us first examine some of the most notable ones.

Scope fluidity

Traditional technology projects usually start with a fairly definitive scope. The scope might change over a period of time, but at any given point of time, it is always quite well defined. As a result, we can develop specific schedules, plan for resources, and estimate costs and benefits. Big Data projects, however, typically start with an aspirational intent of some form of business outcome instead of a boxed scope. They are more exploratory in nature, at least initially. In traditional technology projects, the outcome is quite clear from the outset. In Big Data projects, it is directional in nature until the project matures at the half-way stage or sometimes even later.

> *"Let us take an example to understand what we mean by scope fluidity. You are trying to improve the customer satisfaction for your business. This will help you improve your repeat business and wallet share with customers, which will help grow your business. In the traditional IT approach, you will build an application to conduct customer surveys, capture customer satisfaction scores and qualitative feedback from customers, provide an escalation process, and create some dashboards for your management to review periodically. Such a project will have a defined scope, timeline, and budget."*

> *"In the Big Data world, you can do much more than building an application as mentioned before. You can also create a mechanism to capture data from other unstructured sources such as Internet forums, and source data from other internal systems such as warranty or similar systems. You can do pattern analysis of customer issues based on all this new data from different sources and coming in different formats. As you keep progressing, you can bring more data and generate more insights. The scope of your project will evolve over time as people start seeing the possibilities and capabilities. The new capabilities enabled by Big Data will make the scope more fluid."*

Business case certainty

In traditional technology projects, since the outcome and influencing factors are predictable and quantifiable, it is easy to develop a business case for the investment and create models to handle emerging scenarios through the course of the project. In Big Data projects, there is seldom any business case in the traditional sense that can be developed to pursue the idea. Often, we will do some initial experimentation with data, validate some hypotheses, and decide the next course of progress. This leads to different governance approaches to manage projects and investments. We will address issues around investments and monetization later in *Chapter 6, Managing Investments and Monetization of Data*.

> *"Continuing the previous example, we work with a simplistic premise that if we know what our customers do not like about us and we take action upon that, customer satisfaction will improve and lead to business growth. The business case for such a project is built around this basic premise.*
>
> *The Big Data project we discussed previously allows us to explore more questions because we have access to newer data sources that lead to newer insights. While we go through this investigation, it is very difficult to be specific about the outcome and resulting benefits. So it is very difficult to create a definitive business case."*

Focus specificity

Traditional technology projects are more focused on delivering nicely packaged functional capabilities to meet the defined scope. They are very focused on causal networks for design guidance—what leads to what and how that needs to be translated into the technology solution. Big Data projects, on the other hand, are focused on the business outcome rather than functionality. They focus more on correlation networks—what influences what and what else could possibly change the outcome. These factors drive important differences in the design and delivery of the technical artifacts that are created by the two different types of projects.

> *"For example, a typical traditional IT project will create a system to capture all reported customer satisfaction issues and take them through an escalation process till resolution. In this project, there will most likely be a set of defined channels or mechanisms to capture customer satisfaction issues. This project will specifically focus on improving customer satisfaction.*
>
> *On the other hand, a Big Data project in a similar space will most likely bring together all customer interactions with your business—be it through a web feedback system, call center logs, data captured through structured customer satisfaction surveys, feedback given by customers on social media platforms such as Facebook or blogs, feedback given to and subsequently recorded by your representatives that interact with customers, and so on. This project will also perform analytics on data from different transactional systems such as sales order systems and financial systems. This project will not only explore the capturing of customer feedback and interactions from these various sources of data, but also try to create a context to those interactions and feedback. As more insights are gained, newer data sources will be explored. Therefore, the focus of this Big Data project will keep evolving from recording customer feedback from different data sources to understanding the context of the feedback to identifying the best resolution course."*

Initiation and progression

In traditional technology projects, we start with a business problem, an expected outcome, and follow it up with a functional design that is validated with the business owners, users, and technical architects. After this validation, the normal project management steps kick in. Big Data projects follow a very different path. They generally start with data correlation design and continue experimentation with data permutation and combination till the designers or data scientists see some light at the end of the tunnel on how to achieve the desired business outcome. Only after reaching such a stage will Big Data projects look at the functionality to be delivered to support the business outcome.

Learning tolerance

Predictability is central to the success of traditional technology projects, but this is not the case for Big Data projects, where we are regularly oscillating between possibilities and probabilities. Hence, we have very low learning tolerance in traditional technology projects compared to Big Data projects where it is much higher. The processes in the former type of projects are designed to eliminate mistakes; in the latter type, mistakes or learning experiences are in fact encouraged so that new possibilities can be uncovered. There is an inherent expectation from most, if not all, traditional technology projects to strive for perfection at every stage—clarity of requirements, definitiveness of business case, details of the project plan, and perfectly executed technical code. For Big Data projects, we usually recommend the mantra *perfection can be postponed, progress can't be* (at least to begin with). Let me stress that we are talking about perfection being postponed, not bypassed. While managing Big Data projects, our focus has to be more around continuous improvement and learning from the previous iteration rather than trying to get to the most ideal situation from the get-go.

Data complexity

Data complexity in Big Data Analytics is significantly higher compared to traditional technology projects. Development of Big Data was driven by the following two primary forces:

> ➤ Quest to find greater value in data
> ➤ Limitations of traditional technologies to handle the volume and complexity of data

Large data warehousing projects or massive parallel processing initiatives tackle some of these forces, but beyond a certain scale and diversity, they start showing limitations.

The inherent data complexity in Big Data projects require more unraveling around data that is required upfront. This drives many differences in the methodologies to be followed for the two different types of projects. The differences are more visible in the design and validation stages of the projects.

Functional transaction processing

Normally, Big Data projects will not have many features and functionalities around business transaction processing; the processing in this case is around data. Most traditional technology projects exist to enable more efficient transaction processing capabilities for businesses, thereby creating decision-support systems and enabling new business insights. This requires a significantly higher consideration of user perspective in the design of the application and tools in traditional technology projects compared to Big Data projects, which are more back-office oriented. In traditional technology projects, intuitive user-experience design is critical; in Big Data projects, adaptive data management design is critical.

Defining unique success criteria

In traditional technology projects, the usual success criteria for the project include meeting the business case objectives, that is, being able to meet the expected returns from the investment. Success criteria in such projects also include a compliance to schedule, cost, and quality targets. Such projects have been around for many decades now. Project management principles and practices are well established. In the case of Big Data projects, most of these points do not hold true. From the discussion in the previous section, it is clear that Big Data projects need to be viewed and managed differently from normal technology projects. Therefore, they must be qualified with different criteria of success.

Since this topic of Big Data is hardly a few years old, the practices and principles certainly cannot be considered to be very well established. There are no golden rules or a set of criteria that are sacrosanct. We will evolve as we go along. Previously, we discussed that a Big Data project should:

> ➤ Deliver tangible business value

> ➤ Provide new insights around new revenue streams or operational process improvements

> ➤ Establish new data and process relationships

Use these factors for measuring your success criteria.

We have seen some companies measure the volume of their big data and their growth as a success criterion. This is a very interesting metric but has little value beyond any anecdotal use. You should always monitor the size of Big Data you are managing, but its growth is not necessarily a good indicator of any benefit coming out of it. Any Big Data initiative—big or small—needs to create tangible business value.

There is one size-related metric that you can measure, but this can be done more at an enterprise level rather than at an individual project level, that is, the total storage cost of all data. You should do this in case you decide to migrate all your data storage, management, and processing using Big Data technologies in future.

Creating an Explore, Validate, Amplify framework for Big Data Analytics projects

Projects related to Big Data have to deal with a lot of ambiguity, evolution, and experimentation. Established project management methodologies are less effective in this scenario because they work on principles of a high degree of certainty and structure. There are some very good elements of discipline, which standard project management methodologies require. These traditional methodologies also delve into some very important subject areas such as risk management, communication, change management, and so on. In this section, we will introduce you to a framework of **Explore-Validate-Amplify (EVA)**, which you might find useful for phasing your Big Data projects. In this approach, we take a progressive investment approach and ideate, validate, and refine it before we plunge into any large-scale development effort.

Explore

You have a Gold Coin idea, and you have some thoughts about what data is required to cultivate the idea. You also have a general sense of what business purpose this idea serves and how the benefits could help your business. Now, you want to develop a project to take this idea through to execution. You start by proving that your idea is a valid one and delivers actual business value. This stage is called the **Explore** phase. The objective of this phase of the project is to determine whether the idea works or not and if you have the right data and analytical models to make the idea work. At this stage, you should avoid any temptation to explore enterprise-wide usability and create bigger business benefits. Since Big Data is such an evolving space, it is critical to be disciplined about taking smaller steps quickly as opposed to attempting to solve all problems together.

Building use cases

Your first action in this phase of the project should be to build a use case, which is a set of exploratory hypotheses that support your idea and use the data in consideration. You can identify use cases based on many factors—your understanding of the business, tribal knowledge about the business opportunities and challenges in the organization, and input from experts or customer feedback. Sometimes, even a cursory glance of the data gives you ideas about use cases. Build the use cases by communicating with the key stakeholders of your business. This helps improve engagement of these stakeholders in subsequent phases.

Identifying data sources

In *Chapter 1*, you built an Information Catalog, and in *Chapter 2*, *Creating an Opportunity Landscape and Collecting Your Gold Coins*, you built a Data Catalog. Now, you need to identify what data you need and from which sources to further build your hypotheses. You may be able to get the same data from multiple sources, but you need to make an informed decision on which data to use, or if you choose to consider the same data from multiple sources, how you will mediate between any differences.

When identifying the data sources, you need to understand a few qualifiers about it:

> ➢ What format is it available in—structured, unstructured, or streaming?
> ➢ Where is it coming from, what is the originating source?
> ➢ How does the data get created in the first place—is it manually entered or created by a process?
> ➢ At what frequency is the data created and stored?
> ➢ How and where is it stored?
> ➢ What is the reliability of the data quality?

Answering the above questions will help you gain comprehensive knowledge about your data. This understanding will make it easier to build the Big Data platform and your analytics.

Ingressing data

Now, you not only have an idea, you also have some use cases around the idea and knowledge about what data to exploit to build those use cases. You now need to go ahead and get the data. **Data ingress** is defined as the process of getting data in. This also includes the steps required to authenticate the incoming data. The questions we explored in the previous step will help us define the source of data, how to process it, and how to validate it for the data ingress process.

As part of the ingress process, you need to decide how and where you are going to store the incoming data. At this point, you may not have a large robust infrastructure for your Big Data initiative, but you have many technology choices to accomplish this task. In the next chapter, we will talk more about some of these choices.

Deciding your analytics models

Now that you have your data and ideas about what outcome(s) you are looking for, you build your analytical models. You usually start with classification, clustering, and correlation analysis of data. If you are working with a small data set or a very simple problem, these might be adequate. For more analysis or very large data sets, you may need to use other statistical modeling tools such as the following ones:

➤ Regression analysis
➤ Time series analysis
➤ Bayesian networks
➤ Weibull analysis
➤ Kolmogorov-Smirnov tests
➤ Multi-dimensional scaling
➤ Factor analysis

Make a note

You can get an overview about these and many other models for statistical analysis at www.statsoft.com, an electronic statistics textbook. There are several good books that can help you develop an in-depth understanding of them; my personal favorites are:

Advanced Statistical Methods for the Analysis of Large Data-Sets by Di Ciaccio, Agostino, Coli, Mauro, Angulo Ibanez, and Jose Miguel

Understanding Advanced Statistical Methods by Peter Westfall and Kevin Henning

Encyclopedia of Mathematics by Michiel Hazewinkel

Data Mining: Practical Machine Learning Tools and Techniques by Ian H Witten and Eibe Frank

Beautiful Data: The Stories Behind Elegant Data Solutions edited by Toby Segaran and Jeff Hammerbacher

The choice of which models to use depends on your needs. Some of these models are more popular in certain industry segments. For example, Weibull analysis is used extensively in the insurance claims industry. You can explore using multiple models to get different perspectives about your problem.

Applying analytical models on your selected data sets

Now you have ideas, use cases, data, and analytical models to corroborate the ideas. Your next step is to apply your analytical models on the data you have selected from your business.

Testing your hypothesis

Now you have the results after applying the analytical models on your selected data sets. You need to confirm whether your original hypothesis is correct or needs some further tuning. At this stage, you can also review the aptness of your data sets and the precision of your findings, both of which will help you further refine your project for the next stage. Your starting hypothesis may also turn out to be largely off-base and incorrect; in that case, try to find out why.

Validate

As an outcome of the activities in the Explore phase, you will be able to determine whether you are on the right track in your pursuit or not. This is the stage where, with minimal resources and investments, you make the decision to proceed further or not. For Big Data projects, it is critical that you are ready for your initial hypotheses to be challenged by the data and analytics process. There may not always be an obvious right answer; you may have to go through multiple iterations, and many permutations and combinations of your hypothesis, data, analysis, and results to arrive at the most likely scenarios.

In the validate phase, you go through an iterative process where you run these multiple iterations. In this stage, you also expand the scope of both your testing and coverage. This should hopefully help you to uncover more opportunities.

Identifying more data sets

Let's first assume that your initial hypotheses are mostly true for the scenarios and data you selected. Now, identify more data sets to investigate whether your assumptions and postulation are true on a broader business scenario. If the results of your test from the Explore phase are not very encouraging, check whether a different data set leads you to the same or a different result.

Retesting your use case

Once you have more data sets, you can go through similar steps as you did in the Explore phase and test your original hypotheses with more data. The results will tell you that you have struck gold with your original idea and supporting hypothesis for the idea because any amount of data leads to the same conclusion, or the results will tell you that with more data how your hypotheses change. In either scenario, you are close to firm use cases.

Identifying adjacent data types, sources, and data sets

Next, you need to check whether different types or sources of data change the hypothesis in your use case. This will strengthen the validity of your Gold Coin idea. This step is critical to understand these influences and eliminate any noise or bias that may arise in the outcome of the data and analytics.

Refining and extending your use case

Now that you have a valid use case through multiple iterations of building use cases, identifying data, building analytical models, applying these models on the data, and testing your hypotheses, armed with your experiences and learning, you can refine your use case to arrive at a final one. In doing so, you may end up refining your original use case to either broaden or reduce the scope and hypothesis.

Validating your modified use case

You are almost ready to make your idea big. Now, you have a solid use case, an established business need, lots of data, analytical models, and results of applying those models on different types and sizes of data. Since you have gone through so many iterations and changes, it is good for you to take stock of everything you have done and perform one final validation with all-inclusive data and analytical models. This becomes the foundation for you to make a robust business case for amplification.

Identifying output data needs

Your analysis will create some output data that is useful for further processing or communicating insights. Before you exit the Validate phase, identify such output data. In the Big Data world, the process of output data leaving your system is called **data egress.**

Amplify

Till now, you have gone through some quick cycles of ideation, development, and validation. Now, you are ready to take your ideas forward; you have entered the phase of amplification. In this phase, you take the enterprise or a broader part of your business in consideration and build the entire infrastructure and processes in a robust and sustainable mode that can grow over a period of time.

Building an enterprise data model

Now, you build your enterprise data model. To do so, you can perform the following steps:

> ➤ Identify all sources of data with a similar theme across the company, such as customer identifying data, sales data, and so on. Use the Data Catalog and Information Catalog you have previously built.

> ➤ Classify your data properly. This is also referred to as building a data taxonomy.

> ➤ Keep the taxonomy as flexible and inclusive as possible; this will help you later in using the data model more effectively.

> ➤ Create a very large visual display of this model in your team workspace(s), by using large printed sheets, for example. Also, capture any metrics that you have found through your validation process and show it along with the data. This will trigger many new ideas through undiscovered relationships.

Refining the ingress process

You have already gone through the ingress process in the Explore phase and expanded it during the Validate phase. For the Amplify phase, you need to define and develop a long term sustainable data ingress process. The following actions are helpful in doing so:

> ➤ Enable your ingress process to accommodate all different types, formats, frequency, and sources of data

> ➤ Accept data even if high reliability is in question; Big Data helps address fidelity issues

> ➤ Flag and escalate every time there is data transmission loss so that the impact can be evaluated by the technical maintenance team

> ➤ Retain the rawness and native state of the incoming data as much as possible, unless you have specific requirements for aggregation and refinement

> ➤ Test your ingress process for volume, variety, and performance to make it robust

Developing a functional user prototype

Up until now, most of your developmental artifacts including the analytical models and statistical tools have been limited to your data analytics team. Your Gold Coin project takes some input data (ingress), stores and manages huge volumes and variety of data, processes it using advanced statistical models, and creates some output data leading to insights; this whole process is too complex and time-consuming for average business users. There is a complex technical infrastructure supporting this entire ecosystem. You have shared only the outcome and insights with your business users. If you want to make your Big Data idea or the Gold Coin valuable in the long term rather than for a one-time analysis, you need to develop something which business users can utilize on an ongoing basis.

Before you develop the full application package, you need to develop a navigational prototype of the same. A navigational prototype gives you a good understanding of how the system will work and what some of its features and capabilities are, without investing in developing all the underlying technical components. This is like a series of fast-moving screenshots, which gives the user a look and feel of the system. Navigational prototypes are very useful in seeking good user input for any technology package development because it allows them to actually visualize the final input instead of trying to interpret from a document.

Developing repeatable analytical algorithms

In the Explore phase, you developed your analytical algorithms; you may have improved them further during the Validate phase. Now, you need to ensure that your algorithms are sturdy enough to withstand the vagaries of enterprise data. This involves many considerations. Your algorithm should be able to handle variations in data and business scenarios. At this stage, you should also ensure that your algorithm is a self-learning one and improves its prediction confidence progressively. This process is called **training the algorithm**, so that it can benefit from more data over a period of time. This is the step when you try to make your algorithm generic enough for reusability in other use cases and Gold Coin projects.

Developing an application package

The application package is a software program that delivers your Gold Coin project or Big Data idea. Take your data ingress routines, data storage and retrieval processes, and analytical algorithms, and translate them into a programming language that the software systems can understand and use. Next, create an intuitive user interface for your business folks to understand the data analytics better and obtain insights from. Now, develop any data egress components. In the earlier steps, you have already developed and validated the navigational prototype, which becomes the baseline for the user interface. In developing the application package, you will follow normal software development and testing processes; this part is not very different from Big Data projects and other traditional projects; the differences are more in the preceding and succeeding steps.

Hosting your data and application

Now you have to figure out where and how you are going to host your data and applications. Big Data technologies make this process very easy and inexpensive. There are a number of solutions for hosting, some of which we will discuss in the next chapter. You can choose to host the data in-house or use the services of a third-party cloud-hosting provider. In the early days of cloud hosting, there were lingering concerns around data security and ownership; today, the industry has matured enough to address these concerns meaningfully, making third-party cloud hosting a viable option. Your decision should be based on two primary factors—economics and internal capabilities. We have seen that both options are feasible under different circumstances.

Sometimes, we have seen companies with good IT infrastructure management capabilities procure hardware inexpensively, depreciate it over many years to further reduce cost impact, and build pilot Big Data infrastructure in-house. This approach allows such companies to learn important infrastructure management skills and be better prepared to work with external vendors, should the organization's direction change later. Whichever path you choose, you need to bring all the stakeholders on-board with the rationale of your decision.

Developing a user guide

In today's world of glitzy agile development, many people consider user guides as passé. In the case of Big Data projects, they have gained a lot of prominence. You are in uncharted waters, and you do everything to create new benefits for your business and business users. However, as the capabilities, processes, and technologies that we are talking about are new, your users and business stakeholders find it difficult to understand everything you are doing. A good user guide helps bridge that gap.

The user guide should not be limited to only explaining what the application package is doing. It should also explain what and how data is being used, which analytical models and algorithms are being used and how, how to interpret the insights and act upon them, how to track the benefits, and what to do when you see anomalies; in short, make your user guide as comprehensive and descriptive as possible. Your user guide will also act as a good training material for future similar projects. You can develop the user guide using simple Microsoft Office tools or use some of the more flashy solutions available; what is important is that the content is very detailed and easy for the reader to navigate. In the user guide, you should also mention how to keep it updated with new learning and changes.

Developing a communication package

Sometimes, people mistake a user guide as a substitute for a communication package; it is no doubt an important artifact used in the communication process. Your communication package needs to include more details about the process, which we will discuss in *Chapter 8, Driving Communication Effectively*.

In short, your communication package needs to include why you did this project, what business problem are you solving using data and analytics, who are the beneficiaries, how will they benefit, how to use the application, and how to provide feedback to the data analytics team for further assistance and improvements. The primary purpose of your communication package is to engage your different stakeholders and align them to the Big Data program of your business.

Establishing a governance model

So far in this chapter, we have discussed different drivers, success criteria, and project management methodologies for Big Data projects. With all of these differences, it is important that we govern these projects differently as well.

In a normal technology project, we will typically have a project team that comprises of some business analysts, architects, developers, testers, and documentation specialists, all managed by a project manager. If there are many members in the project team, there will be hierarchies of team leaders and managers. Often, a very large project that spans across a very long time period and multiple departments, and involves a large number of people, gets designated as a program. In such an event, the program is usually broken up into several projects. The program will have another level of hierarchy supervised by a program manager and supported by some additional people who help with aggregation activities around governance and deployment activities. Most large projects will have a sponsor and a steering committee to oversee the progress and facilitate any additional support that the teams might need. In these projects, the structures, roles and responsibilities, and authorities of the constituent members are very clearly defined. As part of the governance process, there are frequent team meetings, weekly status updates, monthly steering committee reviews, budget reviews, and risk reviews. This kind of regimentation works very well because there is certainty of objectives and outcome; in fact, the structure helps achieve certainty.

In Big Data projects, this type of governance model will clearly not work. You need to build a more agile and adaptive governance model. First of all, you need to build a complete flat organizational structure for your project team. The role of your project manager should be equivalent to that of a catalyst for new ideas and new approaches and that of a cheerleader for the team. We will discuss more about the team and profiles of people in *Chapter 5, Building a Winning Team*. You should have no bureaucracy or hierarchy in the team. The team should be ideally co-located physically or using technology. The project should be organized in work streams and iterations. The team should meet as often as required and have free-flowing updates to keep everybody up to speed and seek each other's help in making progress in the different work streams.

The team should engage with and update the sponsors of the initiative frequently to update them of the progress and seek further support. The sponsors and other business stakeholders should continuously probe the team on the business benefits and use cases. They should use these interaction opportunities to learn about the new insights and see how these can be applied to grow the business and improve operations.

The governance process should focus heavily on ensuring that proper cataloging of data, information, insights, business processes, and project artifacts is occuring, and that most of the things being developed are reusable beyond current intent. Our experience says that most Big Data projects are impatient to prove a use case, establish a business benefit, develop the data and analytics program to support it, and quickly move on to the next business problem. So, long term sustenance has to be high on the radar of the governance process.

Periodic focused reviews for Big Data Analytics projects:

> ➤ Data management
> ➤ Analytics and insights
> ➤ Business benefits
> ➤ Technical infrastructure
> ➤ Platform sustainability

We also recommend that you use some kind of corporate social media collaboration platform to manage all communication and activities within the team. The team is bound to go through some accelerated learning experiences about the business and learn how to apply some cutting edge technology in solving invisible and difficult business problems. Using traditional techniques such as meeting minutes, task lists, progress reports, etc. captured on Word documents or Excel files is inadequate because institutional learning is lost as people move on. Such an operational platform should ideally be part of the overall data analytics platform so that all knowledge and artifacts reside together. There are many choices for such a collaborative work platform. We do not recommend any specific one; choose the one which best suits your budget, needs, and culture.

In any initiative, it is important to have a structured process and routine to monitor success. The same is true for Big Data projects. In Big Data projects, this process should focus on reviewing how learning is being absorbed in the team and in the business in addition to checking for progress and compliance.

Treating customer-facing applications differently

Usually, Big Data projects are internal-facing. However, every now and then, you will have a Gold Coin idea that will end up in a customer-facing application. In many cases, some part of the output from your Gold Coin idea will end up facing the customer. There are two very important considerations for all such applications—protecting your intellectual property and delivering an exceptional user experience.

Intellectual property protection

In every Big Data project, there is, as you would expect, a wealth of information about your business, which is your competitive differentiator—your secret sauce for success. The inner workings of your business are captured in these projects. If customers, and possibly competitors, get access to this, this could cause real damage to your business.

To protect your intellectual property, you need to take care that none of the inner workings in your application package are exposed to the user. None of your data ingress routines, data storage processing programs, and analytical algorithms should be visible or accessible to the external end users. They should get access only to the analysis and insights that are relevant to them. You should also try and avoid giving any analytical deep dive capabilities on exposed data to people from outside your organization as well; if you are the one presenting all the capabilities and wrapping your services around them, your customers will depend on you more.

User experience excellence

In today's world of consumer-driven technology, people have come to expect a very differentiated and targeted user experience. The decidedly modern fact of information and data overload and the fast pace of today's world has, it is often claimed, reduced attention spans significantly. Most of the work around data and analytics is very scientific in nature and can be construed as being quite 'nerdy'. To secure and sustain people's attention, you need to have some flashy and attractive features in the parts of your application package that your business users will be exposed to. While you have developed very detailed manuals, there is little propensity in people to read through them; therefore, your application package must be very intuitive. In your development cycle, you also need to keep mobility requirements in consideration.

A comprehensive approach for building an organizational Big Data Analytics infrastructure

In your pursuit of Big Data solutions, there are two major parallel streams—individual Gold Coin projects and building the enterprise Big Data analytics platform. So far, the frameworks and methodologies that we have discussed work very well for individual Gold Coin projects. For the enterprise platform, you need some additional considerations. These factors will help you expand the platform to meet future enterprise needs, make it more robust, induce increased flexibility, and improve adaptability to various new business areas and use cases. While you work tirelessly to make your Gold Coin projects very successful, keep in mind the comprehensiveness of the platform you are building for your enterprise needs.

In this section, we will review some of the key factors you need to put special focus on from the enterprise perspective. We have discussed the mechanics of most of them in the earlier sections, so please read this in conjunction with our earlier description.

The enterprise data map

You have already started building your data catalogs. You need to expand that catalog for the enterprise. You need to start defining a common taxonomy, building data models, identifying interrelationships between different data elements, and spot their locations and other metadata attributes such as format, size, variety, validation, and so on. With each completed Gold Coin project, you need to update your enterprise data map; every time you embark on a new idea, review this data map first. You should identify one person in your team and a backup who will own this data map and be responsible for its upkeep. You should also keep publishing this data map to your project teams, key stakeholders, and other interested parties frequently; this will help with their education about how your business uses data, and it will also help with generation of new ideas.

The enterprise data ingestion infrastructure

As you progress through each Gold Coin project, start connecting all enterprise systems and sources of data to your Big Data platform. Increase your consumption or data ingress as your needs evolve, but progressively keep connecting all possible sources so that your future needs are easily served. Every time you make a connection, try and pull all possible data, even if you do not need it immediately, into your enterprise data warehouse. This will facilitate easy scenario planning and simulations during the Validate phase of your new initiatives.

Scalable data storage

Your initial data storage requirements might start off with a few hundred gigabytes or a few terabytes storage requirement. As people start seeing the power of Big Data Analytics, more demand for data analytics initiatives will get created; consequently, your data storage requirements will also increase exponentially. Storage is not very expensive; in fact, Big Data would not have been enabled if storage costs continued to be prohibitive as it was a few years back. Also, you can stagger while building your storage capacity as you go along. However, you need to get your architecture right early on. Building a substantial enterprise data map and data store will help in monetizing Big Data for your business. We will discuss more about this in a later chapter.

The analysis engine

Once you have identified the analytical algorithm for a project, you can write it in any programming language and use it; all you need is knowledge of advanced statistics and programming. However, when your project volumes grow, it may be inefficient to take this approach. You should consider either buying or building an analysis engine in which you can code all your algorithms. This becomes a good reusable repository for future use;

this also becomes good training material for new team members. In *Chapter 4, Building the Right Technology Landscape,* when we discuss technology choices, we will discuss more about which languages or tools you can use.

Benefits map

As you steer through multiple Gold Coin projects, you will arrive at business benefits accrued in them. It is important that you build a library of all these benefits and state how they were achieved. Doing so will help you in the monetization of Big Data Analytics for your business and also help you generate more ideas; for now, you will be able to see more correlation between data and possible outcomes.

The platform framework

As you build your enterprise Big Data platform, develop one architecture framework to help you put things in context. The following diagram depicts one such framework, but feel free to develop one that you are comfortable with.

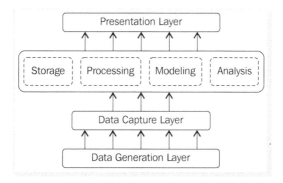

In each of the above layers, there will be multiple methods. For example, your data can get generated from business transactions, human input, sensors, web clicks, and other sources. Your capture for each of these various sources will be different. You can have multiple storage systems and formats in your enterprise platform. You may choose to have a combination of manual and automated analysis engines. You will most likely have many different looking and differently purposed user interfaces. The differences are very important, but having a unified view of the framework will help you remain sane despite the increasing complexity.

Summary

In this chapter, you have worked on various techniques to manage Big Data Analytics initiatives more effectively. In this chapter, you have:

➤ Understood how Big Data projects are different from normal technology projects

➤ Understood how to uniquely define success criteria for Big Data projects

➤ Understood how to avoid the limitations of traditional project management methodologies while pursuing Big Data projects

To manage the unique aspects of Big Data projects, we discussed an iterative and adaptive **Explore-Validate-Amplify** framework:

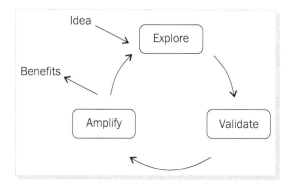

We further discussed:

➤ How to establish a governance model for Big Data initiatives

➤ How to slightly tweak the approach for customer-facing applications that result from Big Data initiatives

➤ How to take a more comprehensive view while building your enterprise Big Data platform

You should adapt the various techniques that we have discussed in this chapter to suit your business context and culture. As we have often reiterated, we are still in the early stages of evolution of Big Data Analytics to have very prescriptive processes.

In the next chapter, we will start building the right technology landscape for your Big Data Analytics initiatives. We have talked briefly about a platform framework in the previous section; we will get into more details in the next chapter, understand the various choices, and synthesize your current investments with future Big Data needs.

4

Building the Right Technology Landscape

Big Data is a vast subject area. The technology in this space is evolving very rapidly. There are already innumerable choices available for you to explore. People often assume that by implementing a Hadoop stack and creating some custom analytics on top of it, they have started leveraging Big Data capabilities. This is not the case. You need to bring together data and advanced analytics using the right combination of software, hardware, and processing components to meet your business needs. We have seen that most executives and technology managers need considerable education on the following topics:

> ➤ The various technology choices around Big Data that are available today

> ➤ What these can do for their business

> ➤ How to apply them in the context of their organization

Leading technology vendors are building platforms and influencing customers on their point of view and product offerings. Each business has different requirements from its data analytics program. Before a single solution set can become generic enough to address a wide range of requirements from different businesses, the available packaged solutions need to progress with a lot more maturity.

This chapter introduces you to the various components of the technology stack in Big Data and provides guidance on how to identify the best choices for your particular context. This chapter also demystifies the commonly used jargon that might have been a challenge for you to understand in the past. At the end of this chapter, you should be able to build the right technology landscape for your needs.

Designing Big Data storage

Big Data enables you to store all of your raw data as it gets generated. For better analysis, it is recommended to store all of the data so that the right correlations can be drawn, even if they are used later. In this section, we shall first delve into how storage technologies have evolved to understand the historical context and put into perspective what led to the inflection point for Big Data. Then, we shall explore how Big Data storage works to get a peek into the inner workings of the technology.

Evolution of storage technology

The history of the evolution of storage technology is one of the fascinating stories in the technology world. In a way, it mirrors how computers have come to rule our lives at home and at work. Till recently, the sophistication in storage technology has been largely driven by the increasing demands from business applications on computing and data management needs. Now, with global pervasiveness of connectivity and mobility, individual consumer usage is driving most of the advancements in storage and processing technologies.

It all started with Herman Hollerith's invention of punched cards in the late 19th century, which was used for census tabulation in the US. This is actually one of the earliest Big Data applications, even though none of the current technologies associated with Big Data were used. In the next 50 years, storage technology evolved rapidly. New methodologies were invented and new types of devices got introduced. This movement was assisted by parallel innovations in physics, chemistry, material sciences, and precision manufacturing.

Some of the key milestones in this journey are:

Year	Creator	Storage Device
1928	Fritz Pfleumer	Magnetic tapes
1932	G Taushek	Magnetic drums
1946	Prof. Febrick C Williams	Random Access Memory using Cathode Ray Tubes
1956	IBM	Hard disk
1968	Bell Labs	Twister memory
1971	IBM	8" floppy disks
1976	Allan Shugart	5.25" floppy disks
1980	James T Russel	Compact disks
1989	Sony and HP	Digital Data Storage
1991	Sony	Mini disks
1994	SanDisk	Compact flash drives

Year	Creator	Storage Device
1995	Philips, Sony, Toshiba, and Panasonic	DVD
1997	SanDisk and Siemens AG	Multimedia cards
1999	SanDisk	SD cards
Recently	Salesforce.com, Amazon, and Google	Cloud storage

Throughout this advancement, a few key considerations drove the developmental work:

➤ Boosting storage capacity

➤ Reducing device size and improving portability

➤ Improving reliability and recoverability of the data stored

➤ Increasing data access and processing speed

➤ Lowering costs

This progression impacted consumer storage more than it impacted business storage because of complexities around availability, accessibility, addressability, mutability, security, capacity, latency, throughput, and finally energy usage.

In the early days, the complete data storage and processing for a particular application used to happen on a single computing device with a dedicated storage drive. So, the need to increase the capacity and throughput of these devices and drives was paramount as demands from the applications grew. Since the late 1970s, some engineers started toying with the idea of using multiple storage drives (could be within the same physical device) for different aspects of processing. In 1987, David Patterson, Garth A. Gibson, and Randy Katz at the University of California, Berkeley, formally introduced the concept of **RAID** (**Redundant Array of Inexpensive or Independent Disks**). They presented their concepts in the paper *A Case for Redundant Arrays of Inexpensive Disks (RAID)* at the SIGMOD conference in June 1988 held in Chicago. In a way, this was the start of parallel processing.

By the early 2000s, the explosive demands for storage and processing was outstripping the existing technology choices. Of the many companies struggling with this problem, Google and Yahoo! were two of the most impacted ones because their business models depended on more and more data; in the next few years, some of the core technology innovations around storage and processing were led by employees of these two companies.

In December 2004, Jeffrey Dean and Sanjay Ghemawat from Google Research published a new way to program and manage data by using the computing and storage power of multiple simultaneous computers in parallel. This was presented in Sixth Symposium on Operating System Design and Implementation at San Francisco, California, in their paper titled *MapReduce: Simplified Data Processing on Large Clusters*. Doug Cutting, working at Yahoo!, used this concept to extend the power of the open source indexing and search project, Lucence.

In the following year, that is, 2005, along with Mike Cafarella, he created the Hadoop framework, which changed the game completely for storage/processing and made Big Data a reality. We will discuss more about Hadoop, MapReduce, and other tools/frameworks in an upcoming section of this chapter. Simply put, they eliminated the need for more powerful devices for storage and processing, ushering a new era of development in storage technology.

Big Data storage architecture

There are multiple storage architectures; the most popular ones have been **file systems**, where the data is managed as a progressive hierarchy of files, and **block storage systems**, where the data is managed within certain specified sections of the storage device irrespective of any hierarchy. In both of these approaches, the data itself and metadata, that is, information about the data and its identifiers, are predominantly treated and stored separately. **Object-based storage** is another method originally proposed in 1996 in the Carnegie Mellon University. This method considers packets of data as objects that contain the data along with some unique identification. In this approach, the larger or even massive data sets are split into multiple smaller components that can be processed independently. The splitting in this method is done agnostic of any inherent hierarchy of the data or its location, thus providing more flexibility of processing; anybody or any process that seeks the data does not need to know the actual location or content of the data; one just needs to know the unique identifier or address. This has been the inspiration for storage technology development in Big Data world. Howard Gobioff is credited with having done a lot of development work around this concept.

In the Big Data Hadoop world, there are two types of primary activities – **distributed data storage** and **distributed data processing**. Data storage deals with taking large data packets or multiple data packets of different varieties and storing them into multiple locations; data processing deals with taking a complex query or action and running it on multiple devices to make the processing faster.

You will frequently encounter the terms **node** and **tracker** in Big Data. Simply consider a node to be a location identifier for data, and a tracker to be a node managing the data-processing activity. There are two types of nodes – **Data Node** and **Name Node**. A Data Node gives the actual location of the device and its component or part (often referred to as server or switch) of the data, and a Name Node stores and decodes locations of all the Data Nodes.

Similarly, for data processing, the main task is tracked by a **Job Tracker**, and the sub-tasks are managed by the **Task Trackers**. The Data Nodes and Task Trackers are slaves to the masters of the Name Node and Job Tracker. All of them can physically reside in the same machine or can be distributed over multiple physical devices. Together, all the nodes usually roll up into a single cluster; for very complex and large systems, you may have multiple clusters, though having multiple clusters within a business area is not very common.

Within the Hadoop stack, **Hadoop Distributed File System** (**HDFS**) deals with storage matters. Similarly, there is a **Google File System** (**GFS**) as well. HDFS is developed using the popular programming language Java. They both have a similar architecture with some implementation differences.

Currently, HDFS is more popular. MapReduce is used as the primary tool for data processing. Data packets of smaller sizes also help in facilitating a much higher number of **inputs outputs per second (IOPS)**, which makes processing significantly faster. The data is replicated across multiple machines at the same time to achieve high reliability. Often, a second Name Node is also established, which mirrors the primary one, allowing for greater reliability. Your infrastructure specialist along with your data scientist will design the complete storage and processing architecture as per your business needs. There are a number of considerations from the aspect of network and latency designs as well, which your infrastructure specialist will take care of. The Hadoop architecture allows for a very high degree of scalability. Facebook's cluster size crossed 100 petabytes by the middle of 2012. The architecture is actually quite simple; the following diagram is a representation of this:

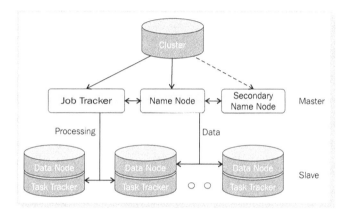

Big Data storage calculations

There are many methods to calculate how much storage space you need and how many nodes you should have in your cluster. To arrive at the optimum solution, there are many factors to consider; the most important ones are as follows:

➤ **Size of the data to be stored**: You need to account for the required historical data and project for future data to be generated for at least 3-5 years; more would be ideal if you can afford and manage it

➤ **Data compression**: If you are using any tools to compress the data while it is getting stored in order to reduce storage space, use the compression ratio

➤ **Replication**: Normally, for higher redundancy and sometimes faster multiple processing, you will replicate the data at least 2 or 3 times in your cluster since the storage cost is cheap

➤ **Intermediate factor**: Usually, some dedicated space is required to store the in-process results of the various processing queries

Always remember to keep some additional capacity since your Big Data platform might grow beyond your initial plan, but this should not be a major concern for you because adding additional capacity is not that difficult.

To calculate the number of required nodes in your cluster, you need to know the total storage requirements and disk space available per device. You should also keep in mind your future data growth, use cases for data analytics meeting business requirements, and any redundancy needs while designing your cluster.

The hardware and operating system needs for Big Data

This architecture does not require any high-end server; the individual machines can be simple consumer grade machines. HDFS, MapReduce, and other components of the Big Data stack will do the necessary orchestration of data and processing between those machines. If you are using consumer grade machines, try to get ones with dual core processors and preferably at least 8 GB RAM. Established IT storage providers such as Dell, EMC, HP, IBM, Teradata, NetApp, and Oracle are offering solutions specific to Big Data; there are many upcoming ones as well.

Most Hadoop clusters run on Linux, even though there are many implementations on Windows and other operating systems. Linux's appeal lies in two contributing factors – it is easy to deal with technically, and being open source, it is free.

You need to choose the hardware and operating system based on your organizational preference and cost considerations.

There is already a lot of published material available that goes into much depth on the subject of computing infrastructure for Big Data; please branch out if you need more detailed information.

Identifying the different technology layers

Now that you understand the basics of storage, your next step in building the right technology landscape is identifying the different technology layers. This exercise will help you in creating a context for understanding the different tools and technology components. In the previous chapter's final section, we discussed a platform framework. In that architecture, we discussed the 5 different layers—**data generation**, **data capture**, **storage**, **analysis**, **processing**, and **presentation**. We will use that as the base framework and develop from there.

In different industries and businesses, data might get generated differently. Big Data technologies do not get impacted by how the data is generated and how it is captured; the major focus of Big Data exists around storage, processing, and analysis. We will now decompose storage, processing, and analysis into further granular sub-layers or activity-groups. We shall modify the previously discussed platform framework diagram for this decomposition; please refer to the following diagram for this. I had the privilege of working with my esteemed colleague and friend Dr. Youngchoon Park while developing this.

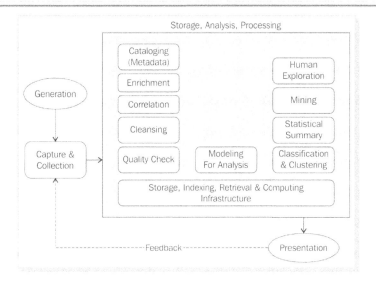

Storage, processing, and analysis are iterative steps, so we will discuss them together. The various activities within that (represented as separate boxes in the shaded part of the preceding diagram) are also iterative in nature. Normally, these activities do not necessarily follow any particular sequence, but for the sake of simplicity, you can consider the activities to start from the bottom and go from left to right after completing each vertical group as shown in the following diagram:

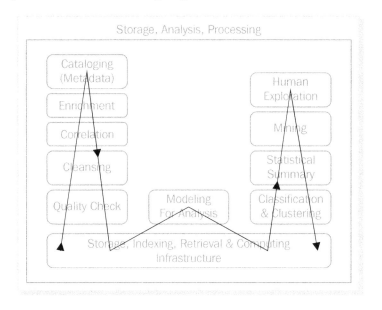

Now, let's understand the individual layers in a bit more detail.

Quality check

This topic started as an academic interest in the early 1970s, when the volume of data started growing along with its significance in computer systems to support businesses. Research activity and framework development around data quality increased in the 1990s, and since the introduction of the Internet, has become an extremely key topic. In 2004, the International Association for Information and Data Quality was formed to be the focal organization that deals with this topic. ISO 8000 is currently being developed as the international standard for data quality.

The primary purpose of a quality check is to identify outlier data samples that absolutely do not belong to the data set. The two simplest checks to perform are validating data lengths and catching empty values. If you get negative values or some data that seems too far from depicting actual scenarios or events, discard them during your quality check. In the traditional technology world, whenever we encounter data that looks different, we consider it bad and discard it. In the Big Data world, we do not follow the same logic; we use it to explore if there is a different scenario that needs to be investigated. Such analyses will get scrubbed out in normal data cleansing and purging practices in traditional data management methodologies. Data should never be discarded at an ingestion stage; it should only be discarded from analytics processing because of the reasons we just discussed; this data could be valuable in future analyses or for a different type of analysis.

The data processing limitations prior to Big Data required extremely high quality data for applications and systems to use them effectively. As Big Data is capable of handling variety and fidelity, other aspects of quality and consistency become less important. Tony Baer, the Principle Analyst covering Big Data at Ovum, believes that "quality becomes more of a broad spectrum of choice that depends on the nature of application and characteristics of data". The real challenge in the context of Big Data is to assess the quality of unstructured data such as text files and audio-visual files.

In general, Big Data deals with probabilities and not absolute certainties. So if you have data quality requirements because of mission critical application of regulatory constraints, this area needs a lot of deep thinking and robust processes, akin to those employed in traditional large data-related projects.

Cleansing

Data cleansing refers to the process of identifying and eliminating inaccurate data from further processing or analytical considerations. This helps improve the reliability of the analytics. In traditional structured databases, data cleansing resulted in the generation of similar data sets for further processing. Prior to Big Data, erroneous data used to cause an expensive negative impact on business decisions because the processing programs had limited ability to handle them efficiently. Additionally, the cost of storage used to be higher as well. For these two reasons, businesses used to store only pristine data. Consequently, most of the cleansing used to occur before acquisition. Not so anymore, as data cleansing is now part of Big Data processing.

While performing cleansing functions, keep in mind a few things:

➤ Focus on finding the noise in data—records or patterns that seem out of place

➤ Never delete any data; today's seemingly inaccurate data might lead to a different business phenomenon tomorrow

➤ Always keep a couple of copies of the data and the aggregated/analyzed results; storage is not expensive

Data cleansing while dealing with Big Data is quite different as compared to similar activities in traditional data warehousing or other enterprise IT projects. Do not start with any pre-built premise that data has to look and behave in a certain way otherwise it is erroneous.

Correlation

Classically, correlation relates to a statistical measure that indicates the extent to which two or more variables or sets of data vary together. In other words, correlation leads us to the statistical relationship between two or more variables or sets of data. In Big Data, we establish correlation to identify which data sets are linked to each other naturally with respect to how their values change and how they impact the same or similar business outcome. It starts with identifying similar data sets. While storing data, if we are able to identify correlations, it subsequently helps us analyze clusters of data sets, making the process more efficient. However, correlation can be used at any point of time for any type of analytics. This is often the practice.

Correlation was first used by Aristotle, but the great English savant Sir Francis Galton is credited to having created the formal concept of statistical correlation in the late 19th century. This is one of the most significant topical areas in Big Data. Since analytics around Big Data works without obsessive focus on trying to identify causes for events, establishing correlations to understand business phenomena becomes critical. Correlations have been used extensively in data warehousing projects, but there it focuses more on similar domains and type-structured data; Big Data significantly expands the scope and variety.

Enrichment

Data enrichment refers to the process of enhancing or improving the utility of raw data. There are a number of methods to do so; the most common method in Big Data is one that combines raw data with other data elements or data sets, which may bring newer insights. Often, enrichment practices also include augmenting the data with additional information like geocodes for location-specific information, demographic data, and so on. Performing data enrichment requires a deep understanding of your business and the ability to put context to the data. This is not a purely technical task. This is also a very iterative process. The key considerations in this step are:

➤ Which data to enrich

➤ What to enrich it with

➤ How to enrich it

- ➤ At what point to enrich it
- ➤ How much does it cost to enrich it
- ➤ How to store the enriched data
- ➤ How to measure the impact of enrichment
- ➤ How to keep looking for further enrichment opportunities

Data enrichment is not new. It has been there for a long time. In business intelligence or data warehousing applications, and even in many other enterprise applications, data enrichment is a fairly common practice. In Big Data, it takes greater significance than others because now you are dealing with a lot of raw data without any level of aggregation; to make the raw data more sensible, this is a key step. Often, correlation and enrichment functions are performed simultaneously as one feeds from the other.

Data cataloging

Data cataloging refers to the process of creating a comprehensive context-specific listing of all data sets that are available on your Big Data platform. In the first two chapters, you took the first shot at building your information and data catalogs. They were helpful in identifying your Big Data play. Now, you need to take a more formal and sustainable approach to building data catalogues that will be used through the course of your Big Data initiatives. It is important to have a good robust catalog so that the tons of data that you store in your Big Data platform can be easily searched and retrieved later.

The context of metadata (data about data) is far more complex in Big Data than in previous data management initiatives. It now needs to combine the business vocabulary of the data and pair it with the information on the structure, format, content, and storage of data. You also need to think about security and access for data because sometimes, many of the rules written around security and access are associated with catalogs and the definition of metadata. Indexing decisions could be impacted by security considerations to make the data easily discoverable, to define relationships between various data elements, and to define relevance. This will have a big influence on the performance of analysis and reporting. Semantics is the branch of study that deals with meaning. Semantic remediation of Big Data starts with your catalog definition. Cataloging is a very involved and iterative process. Do not worry about getting it right on day 1; it will keep evolving.

Modeling for analysis

Modeling for Big Data is an important topic because of the massive volume and variety of data. The rapid growth of such data and the demands for consumption of that data makes the job of modeling complex. Previously, you only had a single physical storage device or at least a single logical location. Now, your data and processing will be distributed over a number of devices.

In traditional data management projects, you had to deal with a lesser number of influences around data partitioning, indexing, and so on; but in Big Data projects, you need to consider additional factors such as search, semantic remediation, latency, near real-time dynamic analysis, redundancy, performance, and visualization, among others. Jinbao Zhu and Allen Wang define Big Data modeling as an *abstract layer used to manage the data in physical devices*, which incorporates all of these considerations.

Modeling in Big Data often involves moving completely unstructured data to semi-structured data to ease search and analysis. As your Big Data landscape grows, your data models also need to evolve dynamically. This makes the modeling exercise even more complex and interesting.

There are several considerations you need to keep in mind while modeling in Big Data:

➤ What are your storage options?

➤ What are the types and format of data?

➤ How frequently and with what methods are you going to update and access the data?

➤ How are different data elements related to each other?

➤ How do you plan to store the intermediate results from analytics?

➤ What kind of data schema do you currently have, and what others can you envisage in the future?

Pat O'Sullivan from IBM recommends that your data modeling needs to start with business definitions. In *Chapter 1*, you built the **Business Catalog** and **Information Catalog**, and in *Chapter 2*, *Creating an Opportunity Landscape and Collecting Your Gold Coins*, you built the **Data Catalog**; these become your guide posts for data modeling. Big Data deals with a lot of sentiment analysis, behavior analysis, and unstructured analysis, so trying to impose a structure early on will not be effective; your modeling will have to account for evolving scenarios and changing needs.

Classification and clustering

Classification refers to the process of assigning a new data object to a certain group or class based on previously defined characteristics of the data class. This technique is applied when the target is known and you are essentially mining the data for patterns. Clustering, on the other hand, refers to the process of combining multiple new data objects to explore any possible relationships between them. This technique is applied when the target is not known and you are trying to run simulations and understand the results. There are many well-established statistical algorithms for classifications and clustering.

While dealing with Big Data, this step becomes very important because you are constantly getting new data and new types of data; you need to find a place for them, that is, which existing data sets or stores they belong with. Similarly, you are constantly looking for new insights that were hitherto unexplored, so you need to keep putting together different types and formats of data from different sources and contexts to see what new insights you gain about your business.

Clustering is very useful when you want to design self-learning mechanisms in your Big Data environment. For example, in a Big Data application for an e-commerce recommendation engine, you cluster past purchases of a consumer to recommend additional products and services. Every time the consumer makes a new purchase, your cluster recommendations might change automatically. If you now associate the buying behavior, or friends of the consumer if you have a way to track that, your cluster recommendations could further change.

Statistical summary for preliminary insights

Since you are dealing with a lot of data and analytics, you need to aggregate your results and findings to reflect on the insights and make decisions; this process is called creating a statistical summary. This is a very well-established discipline; in Big Data, it takes the prime spot because of the huge volumes and variety. Many of the algorithms that create summary statistics have been optimized for Big Data. This is an iterative intuitive process that your data scientists and analysts will engage in. Every time you perform statistical summarization, you should store the results, even if you do not separately store the raw data. This is critical because over time, the context of the same raw data changes, which might be visible in summarization results. This will help you review and refine your understanding of the data, problem statements, and business opportunities better when you look back upon them. In fact, these summaries can also become a data set for you to review!

Human explorations

As the algorithms and tools around Big Data advance, more and more automation will creep into analytics. Today, a lot of the design and analytics has to be done by people creating logic, defining methods and algorithms, and writing code. In every Big Data project, we always make an effort to *train* these algorithms and programs with more data and diverse scenarios so that they yield more accurate analytics. So in theory, at some point in the future, everything will get automated, and artificial intelligence will take over. However, there will always be an element of human exploration because there will always be new frontiers of quests that businesses will seek. Therefore, despite all the sophisticated tools and algorithms, you will still need reviews by experts.

Selecting from your technology choices

There are many technology options that you can choose from for the previously mentioned activity layers. These choices are increasing every day as more solution providers and technology vendors enter the fray, and more development work happens that gets shared in the open source world. In case you have a small initiative with a limited budget or are just starting off and all these different choices are confusing, please do not worry; as long as you have the right data scientist and application developer (more about these profiles in the next chapter) in your team, they will be able to do most, if not all, of the activities using freely available programming languages and software. Many successful Big Data projects started and continued this way for a long time.

An overview of key Big Data technology components

Before we get into the choices available for the specific layers, let's introduce you to a few of these in broad terms of what they are. You will encounter these repeatedly in the following discussion. This familiarization will be useful if you don't have a strong technical background or have been unable to keep up with all the latest and greatest developments in this very dynamically evolving space, as some of the jargon might get a bit out of context.

Hadoop

Hadoop is not a single tool; it is more like a framework that has many components, with several new ones getting added frequently. Hadoop is used for both storage and processing purposes. We already covered a fair bit about Hadoop in the previous section, so we will not repeat it. If you are interested in more details about Hadoop or any of its components, there is a lot of documentation available on the Internet; Apache Foundation's website, www.apache.org, is a good place to start. You can also talk to one of the many experts in this field.

MapReduce

We mentioned MapReduce in the previous section as well. There are two primary steps involved – Map and Reduce. In Map, you take a big problem, break it into smaller parts, and distribute the smaller problems to different workers (or nodes) to seek answers. In Reduce, you collect the results from the various workers, aggregate them in such a way that you obtain a response to the original big problem, and report back the response. While extremely simple at a conceptual level, the design for MapReduce needs to be done carefully so that all the Maps can be independent concurrent operations. There are a number of programming languages such as Java, Python, Pig Latin, and PHP that have been used for creating MapReduce functions and libraries.

Make a note

MapReduce is not a programming language; it is a programming model that deals with parallelism in data processing.

Programming languages

Programming languages have gone through their own evolution in the past 50 years; our intent here is not to review that history. We will list a few of the most popular ones used in Big Data for you. These programming languages are used for many of the layers that we discussed in the preceding section. There are no absolute guidelines on which language to use for what type of activity. Data scientists and programmers use different languages for different layers based on their individual comfort levels and preferences. Later, when we discuss technology choices in this chapter, we will discuss the popular preferences.

Java

Java was initiated in 1991, and the first version was released in 1995 by Sun Microsystems (now part of Oracle). James Gosling, Mike Sheridan, and Patrick Naughton are the original creators of Java. It derives many concepts from the C programming language but has improved significantly on portability and other flexibility requirements. Today, this is the most popular programming language, fueled by the massive proliferation of the Internet and devices. It is a very robust language and has good in-built security features. Programs written in Java can be transported to any kind of computing environment. It is very simple, has object-oriented features, and can handle dynamic features. It is quite easy to find good talent and a lot of open source code in Java.

Python

Python was also built on top of the C programming language and precedes Java by a couple of years; it was created by a Dutch programmer, Guido van Rossum. It is similar to Java in many ways; it has more features that make it easier and intuitive for elegant programming. Python accommodates many different types of programming styles and constructs than most other languages. Python is gaining tremendous popularity in Big Data because of its flexibility, variability, and portability needs.

Pig Latin

Pig Latin is an abstraction language built on top of Java that is primarily used for MapReduce functions. Unlike the other languages that have a broader appeal, Pig Latin is used predominantly in Big Data. It was originally developed by Yahoo in 2006 and became part of Apache Foundation in 2007. This language allows a lot of flexibility in how users define data management procedures while they keep building things as opposed to structured RDBMS languages that are very specific to the sequence and limits of actions.

R

R is a programming language that is designed keeping in mind the requirements of statisticians and data analysts. It has tremendous capabilities in handling complex statistical queries, performing standard statistical test routines, modeling linear and non-linear data, and doing time series analysis, classification, clustering, and other such functions. It can also produce and publish good graphical representations of the data being handled through the programming. It allows software programs written in other languages to be combined with it. It was originally developed by Ross Ihaka and Robert Gentleman at the University of Auckland, New Zealand. Though it first appeared in 1993, it remained in the academic realm for most of the past 20 years. It is gaining increasing popularity because of the strong statistical analytical needs of Big Data projects.

Hive

Hive is the equivalent of a structured data warehouse in the unstructured data world of Hadoop. It uses a SQL-like programming language adaption called HiveQL to interpret relational data structure constructs for unstructured data such as flat files, text files, logs, and so on. Hive has the capability to work with conventional custom programming.

Several data base connectivity components have been developed for Hive to allow it to interact with traditional data warehousing and business intelligence tools. Even though it behaves like one, it is not a database and does not enjoy the same performance functionalities. It is an ideal tool for people who are comfortable with database programming, and it is very good with real-time, on-the-fly analysis. It was designed initially by Facebook in 2008 to combine the power of structured data management practices in a Hadoop environment where it is most optimized.

Mahout

Mahout is a Hindi word that means the one who rides the elephant. In Big Data, Mahout is a set of machine-learning algorithms and tools that help wade through the huge repositories of data in Hadoop. Like many of the other Big Data technologies, this is also an initiative by the Apache Foundation. Its goal is to improve scalability of Big Data platforms and their adoption by making advanced statistical analysis easy and repeatable.

Mahout is a work in progress; currently, it has a robust functionality to sift through large volumes and variety of data to filter recommendations, create naturally occurring clusters of unstructured and distributed data, dynamically classify unstructured data, and identify affinities between data sets frequently occurring together. You can just take the Mahout algorithms and use them in your Hadoop environment to substitute for complex programming.

ZooKeeper

With all of these different technology components and tools related to exotic animals, for the uninitiated traveler, the Big Data world can become a zoo that is complex to understand and manage. However, do not despair; help is here in the form of ZooKeeper. This is another open source Apache Foundation project that provides configuration services, synchronization services, and name registry services for very large distributed systems like those of Hadoop. ZooKeeper also helps improve redundancy and recovery through replication and distribution services. It also helps coordination between distributed processes over multiple physical or logical servers and repositories.

NoSQL

Traditional relational database systems (RDBMS) store data in tables and columns. MySQL and Oracle are the most popular RDBMS solutions used today and have robust data management capabilities built in. They can handle structured data extremely well, but fall short when trying to address the needs of Big Data storage and processing. NoSQL can leverage beyond the relational model and is thereby able to work with unstructured data such as documents, graphs, key values, tags, and so on, in addition to structured relational data. NoSQL is the short form for **Not Only SQL** (Structured Query Language); the name says it all.

In RDBMS, every bit of information is stored as a record, and is identified by a reference key or index or identifier and stored in columns and tables. In NoSQL, even documents or other forms of unstructured data are considered as the equivalent of records and assigned a unique identifier; instead of storing them in specific columns and tables, all records are assigned a location tied to the unique identifier that later helps in retrieval of that record. Carlo Strozzi first introduced this term in 1998 and it was further developed by Eric Evans in 1999.

MongoDB and **HBase** are two very popular NoSQL databases. **Cassandra** is another choice in this space, which has some excellent capabilities in performance management of data storage and retrieval, especially when this happens over multiple data centers. MongoDB was developed by a company called 10gen (now called MongoDB Inc.), HBase is based on Google's storage techniques, and Cassandra was developed at Facebook. All of these are open source projects and do not involve any licensing cost. They all have their origins and lineage in Big Data initiatives. Oracle also offers a similar solution. This is becoming a very crowded market with dozens of new choices coming up.

Other Hadoop components

There are a few other components of Hadoop that we did not touch upon earlier; this listing is to help you familiarize yourself with the terms that you will encounter when you interact with the technical experts:

> - **YARN**: Used for resource management for computing in clusters
> - **Ambari**: Used for installing, managing, and monitoring clusters
> - **Oozie**: Used for scheduling workflows
> - **Sqoop**: Used for performing data integration and data transfer to structured relational databases
> - **Flume**: Used for managing logs
> - **Hue**: Used for developing basic web application interfaces for Hadoop environments

Technology choices by layers

Now, we shall explore the choices as per the layers we discussed earlier:

> - **Quality Check:** In native Hadoop, you can perform a lot of the quality check steps. You can write a number of custom-built expressions in programming languages such as Java and Pig Latin for this purpose. Among packaged solutions, Talend has some promising capabilities. It is very difficult to encode all possible types of quality checks in any off-the-shelf tools because the nature of investigation, along with the course of a project, varies a lot from project to project and can be quite dynamic.

➤ **Cleansing**: Most of the cleansing activities are still done through custom programming because the availability of standard tools is scarce. You can use Java, Pig Latin, and similar programming languages to write cleansing routines. Sometimes, people have used MapReduce functions during ingestion or processing for cleansing; sometimes, Hive has been used for this purpose as well. Of the standard packages, Talend has some capabilities of cleansing along with quality checks. There are several research initiatives in leading universities such as Stanford, MIT and Madison, and WI, which are investigating more repeatable and robust methods. **Data Wrangler** and **Data Tamer** were some of the early initiatives that tried to address this space.

➤ **Correlation**: In the data warehousing world, there is a plethora of tools that help with such activities, but they are not best suited for Big Data. Most of the correlation in Big Data is performed through custom-built algorithms and programs. R is one of the most effective programming languages to deal with correlation algorithms. Mahout has also been used in several projects. There are many good graphical tools developed by the Pegasys project at the University of Wisconsin, Madison, US, which can be very effectively leveraged to explore correlations.

➤ **Enrichment**: Similar to correlation, there are a number of tools for data enrichment in traditional database projects; we are yet to see really good ones emerge in Big Data. The key challenge is to create context for the data to be able to enrich well. IBM, SAS, and Oracle are making promising investments in development and are likely to come out with some good tools by leveraging their traditional data experience and Big Data interest. Currently, most of the enrichment is handled through custom programming in the Hadoop environment; MapReduce, Hive, and Pig Latin are frequently deployed for this purpose.

➤ **Cataloging**: Currently, cataloging for Big Data is also handled within the Big Data environment. Hortonworks has developed H Catalog, which provides some excellent basic capabilities for cataloging. Salesforce.com has also created a robust metadata management capability on its force.com platform, but that is proprietary and not for general usage. You can simply choose to maintain the catalog in the Big Data environment and maintain a more English language representation of the same outside to easily communicate with your stakeholders.

➤ **Modeling for Analysis**: In more traditional data management initiatives, representing data models was relatively easy and could be done with the help of tools such as Visio or ERwin; these are not very effective in Big Data, where modeling is a very statistical analytical process, which data scientists predominantly do through custom programming. Hive is ideal for simple modeling, Java for more complex ones, and Pig is very good for data manipulation. Today, Big Data is still in its early years, and most of the analytics are very different, catering to different unique requirements. Once we see more domain-oriented usage of Big Data practices and tools, we will see more of packaged modeling tools.

> **Classification and Clustering**: Often, classification and clustering capabilities come embedded with data mining and data modeling tools. MapReduce techniques using any of the programming languages can usually meet your classification and clustering needs.

> **Mining**: Data mining is one of the more evolved areas in Big Data with respect to tool support. Since a lot of mining concepts are similar to traditional data management projects, a number of tools from there can be adapted for Big Data; often, they can be directly applied on a Hadoop environment. SAS and Matlab have some sophisticated mining tools that can be leveraged. Mahout also has an excellent collection of components for mining.

> **Statistical Summary**: Statistical summarization shares the same landscape as mining for technology choices. You can do custom programming using R or Python or use components from SAS and Matlab. Hive and Sqoop have also been leveraged for the same purpose.

> **Human Exploration**: Human exploration has only one choice – human ingenuity! Your data scientists and other folks involved with Big Data projects will write a lot of custom code, assemble many open source tools, and venture into uncharted waters. Keep this more free-form to get the best of analytics.

The following diagram is a quick summary of the various layers and some of the key choices; we haven't included solutions from different vendors (unless they have become synonymous with the industry area itself), but there are a lot of good solutions available from them as well.

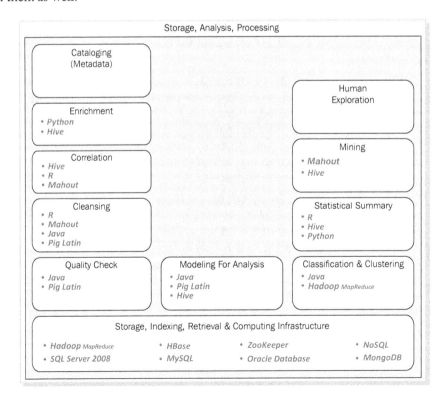

Making the right technology choices

In many aspects of technology, there are a number of models available to select the right tools and platforms; unfortunately, we do not have one for Big Data. In the absence of that, we will provide you with some factors to consider, which will help you choose the right platforms and tools:

> ➤ Organizational policies around the usage of open source software: In this day and age, it is unlikely that any organization will have a formal policy to discourage or disable usage of open source software. However, there might be additional approvals or restrictions that you will have to consider in your planning.

> ➤ Budget and funding: If you want to buy packaged tools, you need to budget for more licensing costs.

> ➤ Programming skills in Big Data: Using open source, free tools and components requires extensive programming in the languages mentioned; take stock of your programming talent in Big Data.

> ➤ Existing platforms and tools: If you have existing data warehousing and reporting and analytical tools, keep in mind their compatibility in the new environment you are building. You might be able to find Big Data adaptations of these tools for almost no cost.

> ➤ Influence of technology vendors and consulting partners: If you are relying extensively on external help, they will try to sway you to their proprietary or preferred platforms, which might involve more cost and complexities but may not meet all your needs.

Creating a visualization of your Big Data

One of the most important activities in Big Data processing and analysis is creating a powerful visualization of the data and insights. Many researchers have concluded that the human brain understands anything graphical better than it understands anything textual or numerical. During the analytical process, you will need to constantly make sense of data and manipulate its usage and interpretation; this will be much easier if you could visualize the data instead of reading it from tables, columns, or text files. When you have insights, your business stakeholders will want to understand those in the context of the data; you need some pictorial representation for that as well.

There are many key considerations you need to keep in mind when developing data visualizations:

> ➤ Which form of graphical representation to use for which type of data

> ➤ How to design a visualization approach that allows interactive capabilities, for example, to drill down from summary value to details with the least amount of navigation

> ➤ How to search and manipulate data sets graphically

> ➤ How do differentiate between insights and data

> ➤ How to develop a visualization methodology scalable with the growth of your data

- ➤ How to address latency issues
- ➤ How to optimize design for high velocity or streaming data
- ➤ How to show data from both database storage and temporary memory storage

While designing your data visualization, think as a story-teller instead of a scientist or engineer or mathematician. Make it easy for your audience to understand the data and insights being presented; they will act on it more effectively.

There are several tools available for data visualization and many have been adapted for Big Data. SAS offers some very good tools for visualization; TIBCO has released a new promising solution in Spotfire; there are many other vendors who are joining this league. There is a lot of research happening in technology companies as well as academia to create better Big Data visualization techniques. Some such prominent projects are Trifacta, ScalaR, InMens, Nanocubes, MapD, and BigVis. We can expect to see more development and innovation in this space in a relatively short span of time.

Understanding the difference between Enterprise Data Warehouse and Big Data

In your Big Data journey, you are likely to get exposed to the big ongoing debate between building large Enterprise Data Warehouses (EDW) or Massive Parallel Data warehouses (MPP) and Big Data. If your organization has already invested in large data warehouse systems, you are likely to face resistance from certain quarters on the new necessity to invest in Big Data. If you already have a data warehouse, you will at least be expected to resolve what happens to that investment with your new Big Data initiatives. In this section, we will tackle some of these questions.

Bill Inmon, the widely acclaimed father of the data warehouse, describes one as *"a subject-oriented, nonvolatile, integrated, time-variant collection of data created for the purpose of the management's decision making."* Data warehouses require data that is inherently structured and of very good quality. The entire premise of a data warehouse is built on extremely structured **facts** and **dimensions**. It is used to synthesize data from different sources to reach a common conclusion or single version of truth. A data warehouse is used more for historical analytics and decision-making based on that; it focuses heavily on reporting and modeling. Big Data, on the other hand, is more predictive in nature; it might also have the issue of accuracy in certain cases. Big Data can also store, process, and manage all your organization's data irrespective of what format it is in or which location it is stored in; traditional data warehouses find that challenging.

The concept of a Data warehouse has been around for more than 40 years now; Big Data is only a few years old. Consequently, the enabling technologies around data warehousing are much more developed, and many product vendors have had many specific solutions, both at hardware and software layers, for a very long time. Big Data started more as an open source initiative; established vendors with lot of research dollars have started creating specific solutions only recently. Once Big Data technologies mature, many of the existing issues around data quality and latency will get addressed gradually.

If designed carefully, your Big Data environment can become quite complementary to your data warehouse infrastructure, feeding it with data from unstructured sources in a fast manner and also possibly reducing your storage costs. At some point, we believe there will be more convergence between the two different approaches. The famous data warehouse exponent, Dr. Barry Devlin, believes that Big Data will give rebirth to a data warehouse. In a whitepaper in 2009, he introduced the conceptual framework of Business Information Resource, which will become a single logical storehouse of well-defined integrated single physical core of data (current data warehouse) and a loose federation of diverse data (Big Data). If you have already invested in data warehousing for your business, keep that going and use it effectively for the purpose it has been designed. Continue to invest in Big Data to leverage the untapped data for your business.

Summary

We started this book by integrating Big Data into your business strategy, then moved on to identifying opportunities, then further worked on a methodology on how to manage Big Data projects effectively. In this chapter, you have been exposed to the technical side of Big Data. There are many layers of technology and an increasing number of choices. Some of the details might be daunting if you do not have a strong technical background. The purpose behind this chapter was to expose you to adequate concepts and jargon for you to be able to make the right decisions.

As a quick recap, in this chapter, you have covered the following topics:

> How storage technologies have evolved and how to design storage for Big Data

> What are the different aspects and layers of technology around Big Data

> What are the different available choices to build your technology landscape

> How to develop visualization for your Big Data

> What are the differences between the Enterprise Data Warehouse approach and Big Data

Unlike most other IT initiatives, technology-related costs involved in typical Big Data initiatives are not of prohibitive magnitude, and they are expected to go down as the industry matures. You can actually develop most of your technology landscape by leveraging open source, free software.

The Big Data technology landscape we discussed in this chapter is a perspective at a point in time of writing this book; it is bound to evolve over the years. Keep watching the social media traffic around Big Data to learn about upcoming technology choices and methodologies.

In the next chapter, you will learn more about how to get the right set of people to make your initiative a resounding success. You will understand the various types of people you need in your team and how to get the best out of them.

5

Building a Winning Team

As we have discussed previously, Big Data brings many new disciplines and capabilities to your business. Many organizations attempt to organize Big Data initiatives in traditional structures and use existing people's capabilities with some training augmentation. In *Chapter 3*, we went into great depth to understand how Big Data projects are different from normal technology projects, and we worked on developing unique project management frameworks. In line with that, your people practices also need to change for Big Data initiatives. Our experience shows that most Big Data projects fail due to incorrect team composition and interplay between team members.

To succeed in your Big Data initiatives, you must bring the right people together in a structure. This chapter provides guidance on how to build teams to pursue Big Data initiatives and make them work.

Understanding the distinctive skills you need

Successful Big Data projects require many skills to come together in delivering them—statistical, computational, data management, infrastructure management, business process, behavioral, change management, and communication skills. As we progress through this chapter, we will be reviewing these skills in more detail. In the earlier chapters, we discussed that delivering a Big Data project requires you to bring together an eclectic group of people. For the team to work effectively and deliver results, you want almost all of them to demonstrate some common traits such as the ones below:

- **Business knowledge**: People in your team need to understand how your business works, in particular, how it makes money, which business processes and operational processes contribute to revenue and profits, how people's actions impact these processes and their outcome, what makes your business successful, what challenges your business is facing today and is expected to face on the next 5-year horizon, the industry landscape your business operates in, what kind of information is captured in which IT systems, and how decisions are made by people and systems. Members of your team should be able to understand the context and the details we just talked about for any new business very quickly; they should demonstrate a knack for acquiring such knowledge as well.

- **An inquisitive mind**: Members of your team should be naturally curious, always trying to understand why and how something happens. They demonstrate a quest for eternal learning. Lack of familiarity with a subject does not deter their motivation or learning process. They will try to find relationships between different events and influences. They will usually not be satisfied with a canned answer to a question without the underlying facts and rationale accompanying them.

- **Intrapreneurial traits**: Entrepreneurs who want the safety and comfort of a corporate environment without compromising on their entrepreneurial drive are called intrapreneurs. Members of your team will get excited with the prospect of venturing into uncharted waters. New opportunities and possibilities always excite them. They demonstrate a strong perseverance to pursue new ventures. They will not be afraid of failures, but will do everything possible to avoid them. They will learn something new from every failure and apply that learning to their next initiative. You want intrapreneurs instead of entrepreneurs because the latter get bothered with the bureaucracy of the organization very quickly and give up, while the former show more persistence.

- **Impatience with status quo**: Your team members have a relentless pursuit to try to improve how something works today. They are not satisfied even if it seems to be working fine today and others seem to be happy with the results. The will get deep into the process, slice and dice it, analyze it, and figure out which components have inefficiencies. They will campaign with management and other stakeholders till the improvements are implemented.

➤ **Visual communication**: Big Data projects are not all about data; they are more about communicating new business insights using data and analytics. Excellent technical skills in sifting through data and analytics alone will bring little or no value to the business. You need your team members to be able to present these insights in powerful visuals that are immediately and effectively understood by the business leaders and users. Joshua Sullivan, Vice President and Data Scientist at Booz Allen Hamilton, suggests that equal consideration should be given to visualization skills. Almost everybody in your team needs to be a powerful storyteller.

In addition to these common traits, you need some very highly specialized skills and people to make your Big Data projects a success. There are many key profiles that are a must for any Big Data project; we will now discuss them, what role they play in the project, what skills are required in such profiles, and where to acquire people with such skills. If you are just getting started or have a very small team, we recommend that you get people with the right experience instead of trying to train somebody from within your organization. These skills are not generic; some of them might sound so, but when applied in the context of Big Data, they are quite different, so do not take a chance on your human capital to deliver your business objectives.

Data scientist

Data science as an independent discipline has evolved in the past decade. It was first introduced by William S. Cleveland in his 2001 paper "Data Science: An Action Plan for Expanding the Technical Areas of the Field of Statistics" (published in Volume 69, No. 1, of the April 2001 edition of the International Statistical Review / Revue Internationale de Statistique). D.J. Patil and Jeff Hammerbacher are credited as having coined the term "data scientist" in 2008 and applied it in the context of Big Data; at that time, they were the leaders of data and analytics programs at LinkedIn and Facebook respectively.

The data scientist holds a pivotal position in your team as they will bring all the possibilities and capabilities of Big Data together to solve your business problems. Vincent Granville explains, "Data science is about bridging the different components that contribute to business optimization at large, and eliminating the silos that slow down business efficiency." Data science is not about a theoretical exploration of opportunities enabled by statistics; it is about a practical automated implementation of statistical tools in creating business value from data. They will take your business problems and make them analytical quests. They will usually be senior person with rich and diverse experience. In your team, you need at least one good data scientist. If you have a large number of initiatives or want to make Big Data pervasive in your organization, you will need multiple data scientists.

Skills of a data scientist

Data scientists stand at the intersection of research and development, and business outcomes. Data sciences cross over many disciplines such as mathematics, statistics, engineering, computing, and business management. The typical skills of a data scientist will include:

> ➤ The ability to see beyond the obvious and find relationships between data, events, processes, people, and how things work

> ➤ Strong knowledge of mathematics and statistics

> ➤ Data modeling, data warehousing, and data mining

> ➤ Advanced software programming skills, preferably in C, C#, Java, Python, and R

> ➤ Experience in high-performance computing

> ➤ Visualization and representation of data, information, and insights

> ➤ Artificial intelligence and machine learning

> ➤ Natural language processing

Your data scientist will have the ability to work with clusters, detect anomalies and associations, and identify patterns and dependencies. Anjul Bhambhri, Vice President at IBM, says "A data scientist is somebody who is inquisitive, who can stare at data and spot trends. It's almost like a Renaissance individual who really wants to learn and bring change to an organization. "Some data scientists have demonstrated hacking orientation; it shows they are trying to break norms and reach an outcome not originally intended.

Good data scientists are also good storytellers. They can paint a compelling picture of how you need to take a fresh perspective of your business using data and analytics. They are not esoteric research scientists; they are very sociable human beings who can translate the complexity of your business and its underlying data into powerful yet simple insights and recommendations.

Of the various statistical techniques, your data scientist will have a deep understanding and working experience with the following methods, which are frequently used in Big Data:

> ➤ Clustering

> ➤ Classification

> ➤ Regression analysis

> ➤ Time series analysis

> ➤ Bayesian networks

> ➤ Weibull analysis

> ➤ Kolmogorov-Smirnov tests

> ➤ Natural Language Processing

Sourcing data scientists

Data scientists are a rare breed; finding one is very difficult and they may be quite expensive. A McKinsey Global Institute report published on this topic predicts a shortage of at least 150-200,000 data scientists by 2018. Currently, more than 60% of the needs for data scientists are unfulfilled; this trend is not expected to alter significantly in the coming years. In the last ten years, there has been a lot of research and writing in the space of data sciences. It has remained a topic of major academic interest with serious adoption by some companies in recent years. The educational ecosystem to produce data scientists is still evolving. There are some institutes and some private organizations that offer courses around data sciences. Many leading universities that had strong program in computer sciences and database programming are leading the pack in offering data sciences courses.

The scarcity and criticality is very well highlighted by Andreas Weigend, Ph.D, Stanford, Head of the Social Data Lab at Stanford and former Chief Scientist, Amazon.com. He has said "We live in a data-driven world. Increasingly, the efficient operation of organizations across sectors relies on the effective use of vast amounts of data. Making sense of Big Data is a combination of organizations that have the tools, skills, and more importantly, the mindset to see data as the new oil fueling a company. Unfortunately, the technology has evolved faster than the workforce skills to make sense of it, and organizations across sectors must adapt to this new reality or perish."

You can hire somebody from academia who has considerable industry exposure working on Big Data projects. They must possess an advanced postgraduate degree in statistics or computer science; most of the good ones will have a PhD. You can also look at other disciplines of studies such as neurosciences, biology, astronomy, etc, which use a lot of data, statistics, and analytics. Many companies have had Big Data initiatives and data-analytics labs running for several years now. Banking, financial services, insurance, security, and retail are some of the industries that have applied Big Data more than other sectors. You can explore those teams as a potential recruitment ground. Start-ups are another good hunting ground to source data scientists, especially if you are able to find somebody who is getting stifled by a lack of funding and initiative.

We do not recommend that you take a smart database programmer or a business analyst from within your team and designate them a data scientist unless they are very proficient in all the skills and attributes we have talked about in this section. We do, however, recommend that you take some bright people from your business and expose them to data sciences courses to see whether they choose that as a career path and help you build a bench, but please recognize that this is a long-term developmental process.

Experimental analyst

Experimental analyst is a new role we are introducing here. In many projects and companies, we have seen teams comprising data scientist(s), sundry business users, and some IT folks. In such teams, we have observed big gaps between the data scientists, the rest of the team, and the business. The project managers for such teams have a very hard time running things smoothly, speedily, and effectively.

Experimental analysts play a very critical role in supporting the data scientists and the Big Data program. While data scientists are extreme technical specialists, experimental analysts are more from the ranks of your existing business teams. They scourge through your business looking for data; they talk to people across the business and find what problems are bothering them; they might perform initial sample analytics to create assumptions or validate some existing ones. Sometimes, an experimental analyst might play a minor sales role—that of setting the context for your project with the business users before your data scientist and project managers explain the benefits and changes from data and analytics that are applied to this particular project. These guys are the scouts and assistant coaches if your initiative were a baseball team. This is a very good role to develop somebody as either a data scientist or owner of a Big Data program depending on their background, skills, and orientation.

Skills of an experimental analyst

Experimental analysts possess both business skills and analytical capabilities. They are very inquisitive people who get restless if they are not able to solve a problem. Patience is not one of their known virtues, even though they will demonstrate strong perseverance in solving a problem. Typical skills of an experimental analyst will include:

> The ability to easily navigate through different parts of your business and collaborate with a very diverse group of people

> A very good understanding of your business and practical exposure in some support function such as finance, supply chain, and IT, or experience with a core business operations role

> Seeking out issues, processes, and related data from people

> A basic understanding of statistical analysis techniques, and an overview of the various statistical models the data scientists are experts in

> Strong communication skills

> Data modeling skills

> Visualization and representation of data, information, and insights

Experimental analysts will have graduate degrees in business, accounting, mathematics, or economics. They will either have course credits and/or working experience in the other disciplines. Many experimental analysts will have worked as solution architects for new IT systems.

Sourcing experimental analysts

Usually, experimental analysts will come from within your organizational ranks. They might be currently working in a finance organization, supporting strategy activities, or acting as a business analyst for a particular business segment or a large initiative. You can look through the personnel of some of the most successful and visible projects in your organization for selection. In the same McKinsey report mentioned in the earlier segment, it is predicted that there will be a shortage of about 1.5 million data analysts and managers to drive the various Big Data projects. You can use this profile to bridge the gap for your business. Training somebody to be an experimental analyst is an excellent grooming program for future leadership roles in the Big Data world.

Application developer

Application developers bring the Big Data idea, associated analytics, models, and business outcomes into a format usable by regular business users on a day-to-day basis. They develop the application packages we discussed in Chapter 3. They will also work on the various data-management routines. Data scientists have programming skills; they use such skills to write and test their algorithms; application developers will help in putting the wrapper around those routines to make them more user-friendly. In a very effective Big Data team, the application developer will do bulk of the programming work, leaving the data scientist to focus more on the data and analytics.

Skills of an application developer

Application development in the Big Data world are similar to the ones for a normal IT project; barring that there are a couple of major differences—the developers need exposure to the new toolsets in Big Data (we discussed these in *Chapter 4*), and they need to have a deep appreciation of how Big Data is different.

It will be very useful for application developers in a Big Data team to have some experience in the following:

> ➤ Handling unstructured and messy data will help in understanding algorithms written by data scientists

> ➤ Handling very large data sets that they can write the correct set of Map/Reduce jobs with performance and optimization in consideration

> ➤ Developing innovative and very consumer-oriented user interfaces

> ➤ Extensible programming (a programming style that works on extending the programming language, compiler, and runtime environment)

> ➤ Object-oriented programming

> ➤ A high-performance computing environment

> ➤ Multi-threaded programming

Developers with package implementation expertise are not often found to be the best application developers for a Big Data environment; their core programming skills do not get used often as the package takes care of most of the logic and mechanics.

Most developers specialize in the database side or the user interface side; some even specialize in the performance side. It may be difficult to get a super programmer who has strong skills and experience in all areas. In such a case, split and farm out the work to people who are most capable of delivering the different components. If your initiative is big, you may be able to afford multiple developers with their special skills.

Sourcing application developers

Sourcing application developers is not as much of a challenge as the other skills, and is clearly not as difficult as getting a data scientist. Most of the tools we discussed in Chapter 4 have been developed based on some existing languages and frameworks. Many old techniques such as extensible programming, which was popular 50 years back, are gaining notoriety again. There is a wealth of published material on the Internet on the various technical aspects of Big Data. Similarly, you will also find a lot of freeware and open source code. So there is a critical mass of people who can quickly step up and acquire the programming skills required for the Big Data world.

You should start by looking into your existing IT team and see who has the skills and interest. You can also hire contract programmers and developers from established vendors or use the services of freelancers. Freelancers are typically more networked, innovative, and might have more varied types of experiences; on the other hand, developers from larger organizations will have the benefits of a larger organization backing them. You can also tap into the graduate students' pool to find people that have the right background and are looking for part-time work. Using whichever method, if you find some good candidates, make sure they meet the criteria of the generic traits discussed earlier.

Try to keep your application developers for as long as you can and rotate them between your different projects. The business knowledge they acquire in your Big Data projects and their ability to contextualize it in their programming will become important to the success of your future projects.

Infrastructure specialist

In traditional IT organizations, there are dedicated groups of experts who take care of infrastructure issues in a shared services model. They have generic skills across various topics related to storage and computing hardware, networks, performance related to hardware and networks, upkeep of software environment, and so on. In many companies, most of the infrastructure support is outsourced with sourcing and some limited skills are retained in the parent company. This approach will not work in case of Big Data projects. You need your dedicated and specialized infrastructure specialist. Big Data resolves problems around huge volume storage and processing of data. It does so by distributing and introducing parallelism in both storage and processing of data. Your infrastructure design and setup is extremely critical for your project to be successful. Trying to run your Big Data projects on your legacy infrastructure is a sure path to failure.

The infrastructure specialist will be responsible for the storage, data traffic, and computing environment for your project(s). The domain of Big Data is evolving rapidly and there is a lot to keep up with, which requires both time and focus. Your Big Data environment requires continuous tuning and optimization, which requires focus as well. Then there is the matter of specialized skills. Therefore, you can share infrastructure specialists across Big Data projects in your business, but keep them dedicated to such projects only. This approach will call for some additional investments initially, but will pay off very soon through the rapid success of your projects.

Skills of an infrastructure specialist

General infrastructure management skills are not adequate for the Big Data world; the infrastructure environment is radically different. Now you cannot just buy some hardware, load some software, connect to the network, validate security, check on performance, and be done. You need to carefully plan for how huge volumes and variety of data needs to flow most efficiently across the processing chain and how the analytical algorithms can be applied most effectively. In this war of Big Data, the infrastructure specialist is your munitions expert as well as your plumber.

Some of the unique skills you need in your infrastructure specialist are:

> A deep understanding of data traffic flows across computing, storage, and networks

> The ability to design and implement distributed storage and processing environment

> Working experience with Hadoop clusters

> Proficiency with extremely low latency / high availability systems

> Knowledge of fabric switching networks

> Competence in ETL products, data integration products, workflow products, scheduling solutions, and system management tools

> Experience with infrastructure planning and design

We have found most traditional infrastructure professionals to be good executioners. For your Big Data projects, you need somebody who is more research-oriented.

Sourcing infrastructure specialists

Like application developers, infrastructure specialists are difficult but not near impossible to get. There are three very good sources to get your Big Data infrastructure specialists from—storage or product companies that have built large businesses around Big Data by providing holistic services/solutions, freelancers or consulting companies that help with staff augmentation, or even your own IT infrastructure group where you might be lucky in finding somebody with the right background, aptitude, and training. Even if you source your infrastructure specialist from outside, it is recommended that you have an internal person also engaged deeply to help facilitate internal processes and coordination.

Change leader

Big Data projects are as much change initiatives as they are data-analytics-technology initiatives. By leveraging cutting-edge technology, data and analytics today enable new insights into your business. These insights often lead to radical opportunities, and realizing these opportunities requires change management. Failing to manage the changes effectively will either put organizations at risk because traditional competition, adjacent players, or non-traditional competitors who use Big Data more effectively can put the organizations' business model and long-term viability at risk. We will have a detailed discussion on change management in *Chapter 7.*

In your Big Data project, your change leader will have little role in collecting the data or analyzing it or putting together the infrastructure and package to use it; however, they help people in your business buy into the power of data and analytics. They are responsible for many crucial activities that are critical to the success of the project, which are:

> ➤ Identify what business and operational processes require change to leverage the insights from data and analytics

> ➤ Communicate with the rest of the organization on these changes and how to reap the benefits of data and analytics

> ➤ Work with business and functional leaders to implement these changes

> ➤ Hand-hold people who have been impacted

> ➤ Develop and administer new learning and development programs required by the changes

> ➤ Monitor the deployment and success of the change initiatives, and make adjustments to the program as required

> ➤ Be accountable for realization of the business goals from data and analytics along with the project manager and sponsor

Your change leader also contributes to more effective working within the Big Data team. They will continuously give feedback to the data scientists, experimental analysts, and application developers on the human aspect of how people use systems and processes today, how some of the new concepts they are working on will impact others, and what features and capabilities might entice them to use more of your projects' new capabilities. They will also partner with the project manager in ensuring effective bonding and working dynamics within the team; you have highly skilled, highly opinioned, and very valuable people in your team; you want them to work well with each other in delivering game-changing results.

In very few Big Data initiatives, we have seen this as a formal role from the early stages of the project. In most cases, change management considerations are left till the very end when somebody realizes that the organization is going to change in more fundamental ways than initially envisioned. Such an approach leads to confusion and delayed realization of benefits; sometimes, organizations miss the bus completely because competition might move faster. Your change leader drives positive energy up in the business to adapt to the new way of life influenced by data and analytics. In most normal large-scale initiatives, change management is more about communication and pulse-checking; in Big Data projects, it is an extremely involved activity that drives the business outcome.

Skills of a change leader

Your change leader is your partner in realizing the business benefits. You need many specialized skills and behavioral attributes in your change leader; some of them are:

> ➤ A deep understanding of your business, operational process, and how people interact with the various processes and create value for your business

> ➤ Good knowledge of how customers of your business, both internal and external, are impacted by the various activities and processes in your business, so that they can put in context the changes ushered by data and analytics

> ➤ Experience designing small experiments to demonstrate changes and drive the impact of those

> ➤ Skills in drawing and modeling operational processes

> ➤ First-rate comprehension of human psychology, organizational behavior, and organizational politics

> ➤ Excellent coaching skills, and who can adapt very well to changing circumstances

> ➤ An easy-going personality but no-nonsense people-management capabilities; a good listener but strong executioner

> ➤ Past experience in driving large-scale high-impact organizational change programs

> ➤ Brilliant communication skills

Your change leader must be a believer in data and a practitioner of analytics. Their business orientation needs to be exceptionally strong, more than probably anybody else in the team.

Sourcing the change leader

Your change leader may or may not come from the ranks of your human resources organization. They will most likely be a business leader who is exceptionally good with people, has all the right skills, and is looking for an opportunity like this. It is best to hire somebody from within the organization; it is easier for them to put into context all the changes. If you are recruiting internally, make sure the selected candidate has considerable experience in external customer- or supplier-facing roles, preferably also with some international experience; these help broaden their outlook and perspective.

If you are not able to find your change leader internally, seek from outside—somebody who has strong change management or business transformation experience. You might lose out on your business' tribal knowledge, but will gain in the other essential skills. In such an event, you need to take extra efforts so that this person gets a deep indoctrination in your business.

The project manager

The project manager brings together the entire program and leads it to the home run. This role is very different than that of a normal initiative where the project manager is primarily tasked with ensuring that the schedule scope budgets are met, everybody is kept in the loop, all risks are mitigated, the necessary infrastructure and inputs are made available to the team, and the team functions smoothly. In a Big Data initiative, the project manager needs to do all of this and more. The project manager's role in a Big Data project is a combination of many functions—they are your quarterback, your coach for the program, your principal sales person, your spokesperson for the executive suite and also the business, your administrator and regulator, and your chief cheerleader. The project manager takes all the arcane ideas and brings the relevant ones to life.

In Chapter 3, we spent considerable time in understanding how a Big Data project is so different and some of the innovative techniques we can apply to effectively manage such projects. Your project manager should be able to implement all such techniques. If your project manager starts to apply traditional project management concepts and cadence in your Big Data project, your chances of success are very limited. The project manager is the fulcrum of the idea and its realization. Your project manager will not only focus on the immediate project(s), but also on establishing the long term Big Data roadmap for your business.

Skills of a project manager

Your project manager should posses the following skills and attributes in addition to the common ones we discussed at the beginning of this section:

- Capability to manage a multi-disciplinary team of specialized experts
- A deep understanding of your business
- Thorough appreciation for how a big Data project is different than a normal technology or change program
- Familiarity with statistical analytical techniques
- Experience with rapid development and deployment methodologies
- Past leadership in technology-led transformational programs
- Excellent communication and negotiation skills

Sourcing the project manager

Finding a good project manager for a Big Data initiative is not easy. The number of successful Big Data projects in the world is still a countable small number (not yet a Big Data problem!). There are no structured programs to make one ready for managing a Big Data project, which exacerbates the problem. If you find a person internally who fits the bill and has experience in leading large transformation programs using technology, data, and analytics, go for them. Otherwise, your best bet is to look externally. Sometimes, bringing a person from outside in such a role is useful to take a fresh view of your business and operations, and drive changes. If you choose to go external, recruit your project manager from an organization that has a culture and track record of using Big Data and analytics for business transformation. We do not recommend hiring a consultant or contractor for this profile since you want this position filled up on a long-term basis.

Defining the team and structure

Now you have a good picture of all the different skills you need in your Big Data team. Make sure you have a clear idea of what role you personally want to play, which could be either one of these or a completely different one. This will help avoid any future confusion or role proliferation.

The next most important question is when to assemble the team. As soon as you decide or have a strong desire to pursue Big Data initiatives, and have started identifying Gold Coins, get started on building the team. *You must have your team before you invest significantly in the technology and infrastructure.* You need to start by identifying the people who fulfil the requirements of the various profiles. Scan the people currently employed by your organization to see whether anybody matches up to the expectation. We have seen many instances where people with the required skills are tucked away in some other profiles in some other parts of your business. Once you get executive commitment for pursuing Big Data initiatives, work with the managers of such people and secure them for your team. If you are not able to staff up internally, lose no time in exploring outside. Get help from the human resources partner of your business in putting this together. They will also offer sound advice on the soft skills and attributes of the people and eliminate any preferences you might be biased towards.

You need to get the team started as quickly as possible. Please remember that they need deep orientation in your business and also need to come together as a team; we will discuss more about how to do this in the following sections of this chapter. These activities will take time, so plan for those before you start seeing tangible output and benefits getting realized. Build your team with a sense of urgency along with the same passion that you have for the prospects and possibilities around Big Data.

Your team should be as flat as possible, especially if you are in the early days of your Big Data journey and have a small team. Each person brings something unique to the table and they need to closely collaborate to deliver results together; you need strong cohesion in the team. There will be some perceived superstars like the data scientists, but make sure you value and communicate the significance of each role to the team members. You must also make the entire team aware of the distinctive contribution being made by each member. Your small team is a band of high impact sometimes high visibility performers who shoulder important responsibilities for the future of your business.

In 1965, Bruce Tuckman created a model for group development, which goes through the stages of **forming**, **storming**, **norming**, and **performing**. In the forming stage, individuals come together to work as a team, understand each other, and start testing each other's behavioral expectations. In the storming stage, people go through disputes and tensions in order to protect their individuality over group behavior and also drive their agenda. In the norming stage, harmony gets created in the team as people develop an appreciation for each other's point of view and align at a common goal. In the performing stage, finally, the group starts delivering as a cohesive high-performing unit. It is always a good idea to take your team through a forming, storming, and norming cycle before you expect them to get into performing. It is even good to encourage conflicts and disagreements among team members early. This will help them get into a spirit and environment of free thinking and free sharing. Conflicts give rise to the exploration of alternate methods and perspectives, which are critical for Big Data projects; after all, we are trying to change the course of your business by doing things differently. These conflicts also deepen the mutual understanding between team members because it bares open their positions with respect to their background and thinking process.

Building an extended ecosystem

You have big plans for how you want to use Big Data to improve your business. If you are planning to accomplish all your goals with your committed but small team, you are in for a big challenge; you may end up short staffed and under-skilled and will slowly get frustrated by the lack of progress as per your expectations. For additional help in getting specialized skills, expert guidance, and expediting your goals, you can build an extended ecosystem and draw upon from the skills and knowledge of that ecosystem. Most companies with successful Big Data projects have leveraged such external capabilities.

Building such an external network requires very different approaches than building an in-house team. Taking advantage of such a network effectively requires considerable effort from your end. In this section, we shall discuss some ideas around building and using an extended ecosystem to further your Big Data agenda.

Educational institutes

In most countries, leading academic institutions and their faculty are expected to have strong industry engagement. They get exposure to various industry segments, and this variety is very useful for upcoming knowledge streams such as Big Data. A lot of the Big Data technologies and capabilities emanate from years of deep academic research. Many of these competencies are based on advanced statistics and innovative computing; academic institutes continue pioneering development work in both areas. Consequently, most of the leading experts in the Big Data space, especially the data scientists, have strong academic affiliations. These experts serve as advisors, consultants, or run labs for large corporations invested in Big Data. Graduate schools are also a rich source for good caliber and affordable students who can be leveraged for grunt work around analysis or programming. These students help build your future recruitment bench and further your corporate brand-building. Building a strong partnership with an academic institution can significantly accelerate your Big Data program.

The engagement framework

There are many types of relationships you can establish with an academic institute; the following are some popular examples:

- **Project-based**: A limited assignment-based engagement when you source some expert help from faculty, use their facilities, and hire some graduate students for part-time work
- **Retained consulting**: When you engage a senior faculty and/or some graduate students on a longer-term basis, say for a year or more, to provide support for your Big Data initiatives
- **Long-term limited sponsorship**: When you sponsor a certain sum of money for a long-term period with defined objectives around developing tools, capabilities, and assets that you intend to use internally
- **Lab or chair sponsorship**: When you commit a substantial sum of money with an institute with broader goals of joint research and development

At any given point in time, you can pursue multiple streams of relationships; this really depends on what your appetite for investment (both financial and time) is and what you are trying to achieve out of the relationship. You can also build a relationship with multiple institutes if you have the bandwidth and want to leverage specific expertise areas. If your team and initiative is small or in their early days, we recommend that you focus on only one institute to start with and expand as you go along.

Whichever type(s) of relationship you choose, be sure to develop a charter and framework for the partnership very clearly. Have a formal legal agreement between your company and the institute; involve your legal department to validate the arrangement. Clearly define expectations, roles, responsibilities, and rights in your agreement.

Best practices

The schools appreciate your money, but you need to devote extensive time and focus to appropriately leverage the benefits of this association. The following steps can help you build this type of relationship:

> Select a school closer to your theatre of action; physical proximity can speed up collaboration.

> Have frequent interactions with the faculty and students to understand their progress and research, and provide feedback; this will also help develop mutual respect.

> Share your problems with the senior faculty and seek their advice; they are not influenced by your organizational limitations and will bring a fresh perspective to the table.

> Define specific objectives around what you want to achieve out of the relationship; this helps both parties work on something of a tangible value and evaluate success in a common framework.

> Engage in joint publication of research findings or white papers, and participate in conferences and industry forums; all institutes have goals around such public representations, and this will help expand your network.

> Protect your knowledge assets legally if your engagement allows for it.

> Create forums for your business leaders to interact with the faculty; this will help reinforce what you have been pushing the organization towards.

Consulting organizations

Big Data has become a large industry segment and is expected to continue to grow in the next 5 years and beyond. Leading global technology services and solutions providers have already built capabilities and offerings around Big Data, and are growing them. There are many smaller boutique firms that have come into existence; such companies usually have specialized expertise and solutions that you can leverage. Engaging consulting organizations might be a common practice for your business already.

If you do not have adequate resources to meet your project objectives and cannot wait to build them organically, this is the right avenue to pursue for additional expertise. It is quite possible that your current consulting vendors have Big Data capabilities; ask your relationship manager. If your needs are not met by the existing relationships, look for new ones.

Before you employ any firm, define what your specific needs are and evaluate whether the firm has adequate capabilities and experience to meet your needs. To avoid future disappointments, do not be swayed by smart presentations and solution frameworks. Demand to interact with the actual people who will be working with you; appraise whether they have the specific know-how to meet your goals. Often, consulting companies will progress their employees engaged with business intelligence projects into Big Data; this approach is not flawed, but those employees need proper training and orientation in Big Data. Sometimes, consulting services companies roll-up their back-office analytical support or knowledge process outsourcing activities as Big Data projects; be sure to eliminate those cases, as the similarities between Big Data projects and these types of projects are very limited. You should use the same criteria as you have done internally to evaluate your vendor profiles.

The engagement framework

There are many engagement models in the consulting world, most of which can be leveraged to structure your Big Data initiatives:

> **Staff augmentation**: When you want specific skills around application development or a sundry analyst or an infrastructure specialist, this is the model to adopt. If you are not sure about the scope and plans around your project, it is best to gather a group of skilled experts and let them figure things out; in such situations, staff augmentation works very well.

> **Project-based**: When your project is reasonably well defined and you are severely resource-constrained, this model is a suitable one for you. Make sure you have clarity on the business problem, data sets, data definitions, expected outcome, and estimated timeline to achieve the outcome before you award a project to somebody.

> **Outcome-based**: If you have specific expectations about how you want to change your business but have no skills or time to invest in that pursuit, you can explore outcome-based approaches. In such situations, usually, the majority of the fees of your consulting vendor are linked to the success metrics of the project outcome. In this model, you might have to bundle some transaction processing and infrastructure-hosting activities along with building the data and analytics ecosystem.

> **Platform-based**: When you leverage some third-party platform to run your data and analytics program and use it in a service-based model with usage-based pricing, it is a platform-based engagement model. This is not very popular in the Big Data space yet; companies are offering only slivers of capabilities. However, we believe that in the future, as the Big Data industry matures, this model will become the most popular one.

The choice of the engagement model depends on how mature you are in your expectations, where you stand in your Big Data journey, and what kind of engagement management capabilities you have in your business. The first two models are easy to manage and ideal when you are in a more exploratory mode. To pursue the latter two models, you need a very deep and clear understanding of specific business outcomes you expect from your Big Data initiatives, and are comfortable not having day-to-day control on the initiative. These models are riskier than the other ones so you will need to have a solid mitigation plan before you pursue these.

Best practices

Sometimes, we engage a vendor, expecting a perfect and quick solution; remember that Big Data is new for everyone, so you need to invest as much as well. When you select your consulting vendor, there are a few things you can do to help you be more successful:

> ➤ Ensure that your vendor partner and the team working on your project(s) have a very deep understanding of your business; do not take relevant industry experience as the qualifying criteria; your business is different

> ➤ Check on the advanced statistics knowledge and skills in your vendor's organization unless you are buying a specific technology solution

> ➤ Create success-linked incentives for your vendor to excite them for greater innovation and performance; avoid normal risk-reward clauses in your arrangement as they might lead your vendor to be extra conservative

> ➤ Become a reference for your vendor if you are satisfied with their performance; you will help them build a sunrise practice and they will put in their best efforts for you

> ➤ Establish which data sets and parts of your business your vendor has access to from the beginning, keeping in mind organizational confidentiality requirements

> ➤ Protect your data and analytics assets through a strong legal framework in the engagement agreement; if the language is loose, your vendor will reuse these assets without any benefit to you; you need to ensure that your legal framework strongly protects your intellectual property around data and analytical algorithms

> ➤ Have periodic reviews, which includes quantitative progress tracking and qualitative lessons learned; this is a new area for both of you; open learning and sharing will help you both make progress

> ➤ Avoid buying any generic frameworks from your vendor; they rarely work without significant modifications, so you might as well do fresh development

An open and healthy relationship of mutual respect between you and your vendor will go a long way in furthering your Big Data agenda. Let them in to help you and they will make best efforts to make you successful.

Improving team alignment and performance

In the initial days, your project team for Big Data Analysis is most likely to be a small one. It is critical for your team to be well aligned with each other and towards the common objectives you have set. Even for larger teams, this problem still remains. You can take a number of steps towards this goal. We will now discuss some of the high impact ones in this section.

Training and orientation

One of the first steps to bring everybody together is to conduct a common set of training and orientation programs. This will help them speak a common language and understand each other better. Some of the key topics you should include in this program are as follows:

> - **Statistics**: Many of us have taken Statistics courses in our schools will remember most of these concepts and use a few of them from time to time. It is unlikely that we will have a deep familiarity with the theories and formulae, and how to apply them on large problems, unless our jobs required us to. Advanced Statistics forms a very key part of Big Data. So it is important that we have a crash course in Statistics once again. Institutions like Royal Statistics Society (www.rss.org.uk) and American Statistical Association (www.amstat.org) offer a very wide range of good courses and learning material to help you with knowledge around this subject. This will help your team start from a common plane of understanding around how to manipulate data and perform advanced analytics.

> - **Data literacy**: Data literacy is having an understanding of the meaning of data, where to get it, how to get it, how to analyze it, how to manipulate it, how to derive information out of it, and finally how to present it effectively. Data literacy helps you build insights with data and determine its value. Data is the primary input asset your project deals with, so developing strong data literacy is important for your team.

> - **Business flow**: It will be good to take another deep dive into how your business works, how data and information flow through the business, and how various processes and organizations interface with different outcomes in your business. This will facilitate a common understanding of the business between all members of your team.

> - **Big data technologies**: Not everybody in your team will be doing deep software-related technical work. The data scientist and the application developer(s) in your team will have expertise in various products and solutions around Big Data. Exposure to the architecture and various technology options around Big Data will help everybody understand the possibilities and options that are available today.

Quick wins

Shared success in quick win projects is another great way to bring people together; the accomplishments give an opportunity to everybody for positive bonding. The framework for Gold Coin projects makes such quick wins possible. On this topic of quick wins, in his October 2012 HBR webinar, Dr. Andrew McAfee advises us to use the rule of 5: *five projects in five weeks by five people*. If you are just getting started, this might be a daunting goal. The idea here is to engineer some successes early, so that the vibrancy can fuel future successes.

Rotational leadership

Each member of your team brings unique skills to the table, and all of them are critical for the success of your project. Like in any other situation, the project manager bears the ultimate accountability for success. Often, in Big Data projects, the data scientist becomes the star, and between the project manager and the data scientist, they all concentrate on decision making. To get everybody feeling equally responsible and vested in the success of the project, and to ensure that all different perspectives are given due consideration, try to rotate the leadership of the group every 2-3 weeks between various team members. We have seen this technique cause some initial confusion and friction, but in the long run, it helps develop a very healthy respect among team members. If at any point, the team is deemed to be getting derailed from its objective or path, the project manager needs to intervene and take control back.

Motivating your team towards progress

By now, it is clear that your Big Data team has a critical role to play in your business' future. You want them motivated and at their peak performance to help you drive your business towards growth. These people are unique and need different treatment to motivate them. The right people in your Big Data team will demonstrate some common behavioral traits:

> ➤ They will not be bothered by organizational hierarchies, even though they will show respect for authority and structure

> ➤ They will not get too excited by normal motivational incentives such as financial or positional rewards; they will be more excited by the opportunity to solve complex analytical and business problems

> ➤ They might be reticent at times, but they like to share and collaborate and be generally helpful to others in the right environment

The traditional motivation theories do not work well with Big Data teams. They live by a slightly different creed. These people are precious and they know it. Their knowledge along with the plethora of opportunities in the world to solve problems with data and analytics keeps them humble and grounded. In our research and practice, we have seen some common practices that help in better motivating such a group:

> ➤ Give them lots of new challenges and give them the freedom to pursue those challenges

> ➤ Make available the latest tools and technology for the team to use in solving Big Data problems

> ➤ Allow and even encourage them to interact with peers from other industries, share war stories, and learn about what others are doing, keeping in mind organizational confidentiality issues

> ➤ Send them to conferences and workshops where they can learn and share about Big Data applications

> ➤ Celebrate each success and individually acknowledge everybody's unique contribution to the success

> ➤ Celebrate each failure and reflect on the lessons learned

Be very careful not to create any artificial organizational hierarchies, reporting lines, and work management processes that reel of bureaucracy. This can be the biggest turn-off for your team.

For the different profiles in your team, different enticements attract them to the workplace. Let us look at a few such points for these profiles:

> ➤ Data scientists are passionate about data. Give them data and they will be very happy. Kevin Novak, Data Scientist at Uber, in an interview in October 2013, says that "If you're a company interested in attracting data scientists, start capturing data now and start storing it somewhere (it doesn't even have to be all that fancy or involved, as long as the data is there it can always be cleaned up later) ." Make an honest attempt to create a culture around data in your executive suite and in your business, and your data scientists will make every effort to give the job their best.

> ➤ Experimental analysts are high-energy people with a deep understanding of your business and how to analyze it. Give them fresh challenges to apply their knowledge and understanding and you will see them shining. Let them interface seamlessly with the business leaders and the executive suite; this will help them learn from valuable feedback, broaden their perspective, and feel recognized.

> ➤ Application developers in the Big Data space are extreme programmers at heart. Frequent interaction with business users and being made to feel part of the business is a huge motivator for such people. Give them all the technology and infrastructure they ask for and do not swamp them down with process bureaucracy; let them change design and development frequently to meet evolving understanding and progressive needs; they will surprise you with their high quality and quick output.

> ➤ Infrastructure specialists have simple needs in life, but they are very particular about those. They need control over their environments, they need to understand the future plans for growth of their infrastructure, and they need everybody to follow the few simple rules they set. Engage them in the analysis, in application development, and in the interactions with your business, and they will go the extra mile to innovate and optimize your Big Data infrastructure.

> ➤ Change leaders need two things—for everybody to understand the significance of change management and feel empowered in driving the change through the organization. Change management is often given a functional connotation without adequate empowerment. Your business leaders and even the project team may not have deep appreciation of how data and analytics is transforming the business, having an impact on various processes, and changing people's lives. Take care of these issues and your change leader will make a significant contribution towards furthering your Big Data agenda.

> ➤ Project managers are generally very driven and self-motivated people. In Big Data projects, they are faced with the challenge of working in completely uncharted waters, which few understand, and where being successful may become an iterative process. So keep giving them reassurances from time to time about the critical business significance of the project and confirm the business support for the project, and they will take care of the rest.

Summary

In this chapter, you focused on organizing your team to lead you down a path of success. You identified the distinctive skills you require for your project—data scientists, experimental analysts, application developers, infrastructure specialists, change leaders, and project managers.

You identified the unique experiences and expertise you need in these profiles in the context of Big Data projects and where to source them from. You then worked on how to put your team together and what kind of structure to put them in.

Next, you learned about how to build an extended ecosystem comprising academic institutes and consulting organizations to accelerate your Big Data initiatives. In this discussion, you worked on defining the right engagement framework and some best practices to make the engagement successful. You then explored techniques to improve your team alignment and make them more productive through training, quick-wins, and innovative leadership models. Finally, you worked on topics that covered how to best motivate this diverse team of yours.

In the next chapter, we will work on investments and financial management related to Big Data. In that discussion, we will investigate how to handle topics such as valuation of Big Data, a problem that is fast becoming critical for your executives, analysts, and shareholders.

6

Managing Investments and Monetization of Data

"In God we trust, all others must bring data."

Edwards Deming

Data has always been considered useful, but rarely has any value been attached to it. It was never an asset class by itself. Big Data is changing this; it is redefining how data acquires and generates value. Until recent times, businesses were valued on their assets, current income, potential growth, and similar financial parameters. Today, the IPOs of Big Data age companies, such as Facebook and Twitter, are showing us that investors are willing to pay a premium of hundreds of billions of dollars over physical assets and actual income for the value of data these companies have access to. Facebook went public on 18 May 2012 at a share price of $38, leading to a market capitalization of $104 billion. Before the IPO, it had already crossed 1 billion subscribers. In 2011, Facebook made profits of $1 billion. So, investors really paid for the potential value of the enormous data that Facebook has about its subscribers. Investors valued the data Facebook has about each subscriber at approximately $100!

There are lots of opportunities for monetization of data. In a 2012 EMC-sponsored research on the digital universe, the research firm IDC estimated that only 1 percent of the available data was analyzed in the world. These numbers have surely grown in the last 18 months, but still there is a lot of scope to analyze more data. Yes, it takes some investment to analyze the data. However, as you are already paying to collect and store all of it, if you do not use it to your maximum benefit, you have lost possible opportunities. In your business, you may be sitting on a treasure trove of data without even realizing it. In this chapter, we will explore how we can unlock some of that value.

Billions of dollars are being spent on Big Data across the world; IDC estimated in December 2013 that the Big Data market will cross $16 billion in 2014, and a lot more Big Data companies are getting generated through new business opportunities or operational savings using Big Data. In the previous chapters, we have discussed how to approach Big Data in a way that is different from normal technology initiatives. Managing money in the Big Data world requires different approaches. We will discuss some of these techniques in this chapter.

Understanding how data creates value

Advancements in computing technologies have reduced the cost of collection, storage, and processing of data; *advancements in analytics have increased the value of data*. Earlier, raw data did not have any inherent value. Once it was processed, the resultant information was useful to take decisions and for usage in other business processes. So, the value lay in the information that was derived from the raw data. Now, we can process all data to create new insights and new businesses. Therefore, the influence of raw data today is significantly more than ever before. Unlike physical assets, the *value of data is perpetual*. The more we use it in varied ways and create newer insights, the more its value increases. In his *Seven Laws of Data Science*, Dr. Jerry Smith postulates, "The value from combined independent data is greater than the combined value of each data alone." Every time we pair new data sets leading to further newer insights, the value of those data sets increases. Professor Myer-Schonberger and Kenneth Cukier have identified the transformation in data's value as one of the biggest changes in moving from a digital age to a Big Data age.

Make a note

In 1999, Daniel Moody and Peter Walsh from Australia presented a white paper in the European Conference on Information Sciences titled *Measuring the Value of Information: An Asset Valuation Approach*. This is one of the earliest practical attempts to address the valuation of data and information. In this paper, the authors proposed their *Seven Laws of Information*, which is a very good read for anybody working on data and analytics. Later, many models were attempted. They ended up focusing more on the cost of data acquisition and processing rather than the value created by it; such models found less appeal for adoption by businesses.

Insights and influence

Data derives its value from **insights** and **influence**. An insight is when data is telling us something new in its current state and correlation with other data elements. For example, we have the customer demographic data for a retail store and sales data by customer for the same store. If we connect the two, we can identify the customers' brand preferences by age group and income group. This is an insight. This insight will help us make inventory decisions, marketing and promotions decisions, and other such calls. Without doing anything different to the data or with the data, using simple correlations, we are able to get a new understanding.

Now, consider that you know which profession the customers belong to and you know how the compensation cycles work in those professions. Usually, customers' profession information is part of the core customer data. However, the compensation cycles are external data not related to individual customers. The compensation cycles can tell you more about when people belonging to that profession will have the proclivity to spend. Now, you have got a new data point and a new insight—a time dimension for the likelihood of spending by people belonging to a certain profession.

This time dimension data will deeply influence your decisions around inventory and marketing, possibly even staffing levels of retail floor associates; this is a further new insight. We call this phenomenon **data deriving value through influence**.

Tip

The value from insight is intrinsic to the data, while the value from influence is derived from the application of the data in more sophisticated ways.

Immediate and future value

Data could have **immediate** value or **future** potential value. If we have an actionable insight from data right away or are able to use it to influence some other data interpretation to create further new insights, the data has immediate value. In the example discussed in the preceding paragraphs, the value of all the data considered has immediate value.

However, we may be able to create value out of data only in the future, because we need either a historical perspective to the data, or we might need to pair it with some other data that we do not have the means to access now. This frequently happens with time-series data—something that is measured sequentially at defined intervals. Very often, time-series data will not give any meaningful insights immediately, but when we look for patterns over a period of time and try to correlate it with other data or insights, we can create substantial value. For example, traffic flow data at a particular location, route, or region for a period of time tells us very little that we already do not know. However, when we analyze the same data from a much larger window and overlay it with weather information, important events in the location/region, availability and performance of public transportation, location of housing and places of work along the route, demographics of people using the route, and similar information, we can start seeing many trends that can be very useful for local governments, town planners, commuters, owners of transportation related businesses in the area, and so on. Not only the traffic flow data, but changes in all other data points discussed here have to be seen in the context of their changes over a period of time to make sense out of them and understand the trends. This is how value of data is created in the future.

Value creation for data

So far, in this section, we discussed how the value of data gets created; we discussed four dimensions: insights, influences, immediate, and future. If we plot the four dimensions in a 2 x 2 matrix, this gives us a simple way to understand how the value of data gets created.

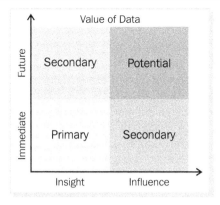

Primary data is the lowest logical aggregation of data that can be the building block for your analytics. For example, a customer's address as a data element comprises of house or apartment number, street address, city/town, postal code, and country at a minimum. If all of these are relevant and required for your analytics, it becomes primary data. By combining multiple primary data blocks, we get secondary data blocks.

Tip

Intuitively, we know that as we combine more data and derive more insights, the resulting value increases. Data scientists and Big Data practitioners have always struggled with the question regarding how much effort they should spend on enriching data. In his article, *Big Data and the Power of Three*, Dr. Jerry A Smith has created some mathematical models to show how the value of Big Data increases exponentially as you keep adding more data sets and insights; at the same time, he also suggests that the change in return on investment starts diminishing after a few iterations. So, depending on your business context, you can decide the extent of enrichment or recombination that you want to pursue.

Capturing the value of data

In the previous section, we discussed how data creates value. Now, let's find out what the value of data is and how to capture it; we will now move from understanding the process to understanding the math. The crux of monetizing Big Data lies in capturing the value created by data as correctly as possible. In going down this path, it is important to remember that this monetization process is not an exact science, so we will have to work with some assumptions and approximations.

Identifying the value

Data leads to insights and insights lead to tangible business benefits. In the example of retail store customer information from the previous section, the data will lead us to stocking and promotion decisions, which will most likely result in new customers coming in or existing customers visiting more frequently and customers buying more. The insights and resulting actions will lead to tangible business benefits in terms of higher sales and profits. It is not very difficult to capture this additional profit as an outcome of data and analytics. This is a very simplistic example, and many of these actions for an individual store can even be achieved without using Big Data capabilities. For thousands of stores across many states of countries, you will need Big Data. Imagine you are doing analysis for thousands of stores and you are playing with hundreds of parameters instead of a couple; the exercise becomes quite complex. In such a situation, trying to articulate the value of data alone will become more complicated. The problem gets compounded if you are trying to repeat this frequently. The difficulty level comes from all the unknowns around how many different ways any particular data can be used and what all it can influence at what point of time. If you are new in the journey of Big Data or have a very small team working on Big Data, these complexities can be overwhelming.

In such a situation, you can take an alternate approach of valuing the Gold Coin project first before you dissect the value of data. A Gold Coin has a reasonably well defined and stable objective, input data set, and analytical models—all leading to an expected tangible business outcome. The basic process of value identification does not change with this approach; you still create a monetary equivalent of the business benefits. There is also the debate about whether data creates value or analytics does. Each Gold Coin project comprises of many data elements and many analytics. So, using Gold Coin projects as a basis to calculate value avoids the debate.

As you keep getting more comfortable with the data elements and their clusters, you can attempt to further decompose the benefits coming from a Gold Coin into what data elements and which analytics are contributing to how much of the benefit. You can do this by disassociating one or more of the data elements from consideration and identifying the impact. However, now you will have to manage situations where the same data is used by multiple Gold Coin projects. Based on our experiences, this happens quite often; for example, customer data is usually shared by different projects, unless you are combining a particular data element with others, which makes its usage and interpretation very different. For example, *customer when combined with location* gives a different interpretation than *customer combined with income group*, you need to ensure that there is no double counting.

At this stage, the most important goal is to develop an understanding that data and analytics create real value. We also need to understand how it does so and get into the discipline of capturing that value systematically. You need to build this consideration into the rhythm of your Big Data initiatives.

Building a value catalog

The next step for you is to build a **Value Catalog** for data. If you are in the development stage of your Gold Coin, the value will be perceived. Once the idea has been implemented and enough time has passed for realization, we will be in a position to capture the actual benefits and, thereby, the actual value. Sometimes, your Gold Coin idea has a finite short life, and the benefits will be realized in a single go: once the hypothesis is proven, changes are implemented, and benefits are accrued; this is a one-time Gold Coin. Let's take a look at an example.

Your business is losing customers rapidly due to satisfaction issues. You can understand customer complaints through multiple listening posts—direct complaints registered through your company's helpline or website, social media posts, reports filed by your employees who interface with customers, reasons to lose customers in your CRM system, and quality system records, among others. You are dealing with structured, unstructured, and streaming data. This is a classic Gold Coin idea. You develop this idea, collect the data, perform your analytics, identify the issues, and fix them in a way that they do not recur; this will become a one-time Gold Coin.

On the other hand, many of your Gold Coins will have a long life. These are the ones where data and analytics can be expected to keep churning out new insights, creating value for a long time. In the example of the x-ray manufacturer from *Chapter 2*, opportunities for repair will keep increasing as the equipment life increases. Most of the examples of Gold Coins that we discussed in the previous chapters fall in this category. In this case, you need to consider the value from a short-term as well as long-term perspective. There are no strict definitions on what is short term and long term; it really depends on the nature of your business. If you are part of a fast moving and quickly changing business environment, your short term could be 3 months and long term could be 3 years; otherwise, you could work with a 1-year and 5-year horizon. Call these the **current** and **future** value of data. Once you have completed the value identification for a particular Gold Coin project, you move on to the next one and repeat the process.

To build the Value Catalog, list all of the Gold Coin projects and their associated values. You can use a table similar to the following one:

Gold Coin	Current value		Future value	
	Estimated	Actual	Estimated	Actual
Gold Coin project 1				
Gold Coin project 2				
Gold Coin project 3				
Total				

In building this Value Catalog, you need to keep in mind a few points, which are as follows:

> ➤ The estimated values can be your best guess supported by logic and calculations

> ➤ The actual values need to be the ones that are calculated after the realization and completion of the assigned window for monitoring (3 months/1 year/ 3 years/5 years)

> ➤ Use the same currency, preferably your standard corporate one in case you have geographically dispersed projects

> ➤ The data in this table is true for a point in time, so keep reviewing it and updating it every 3 months at least; you will also be able to see the movements

> ➤ If there are significant gaps between the actual and estimated values, alert the project team and concerned stakeholders to perform a deep dive

> ➤ Keep your list running from the day you started your Big Data initiative; this will help you get a historical perspective and also help in the future with more formal monetization of data and analytics

As you become more proficient in this process, you can start building the Value Catalog for actual data elements. The procedure is no different from the one outlined here for Gold Coin projects. In fact, we recommend that as you mature in your Big Data journey, do build a Value Catalog for data. This will help in making data an independent asset class and, possibly, increase the valuation of your company. Higher valuation will increase your investment bandwidth, and you can accelerate your Big Data initiatives!

Understanding and capturing your Big Data costs

Big Data does not necessarily mean big costs; in fact, it is the other way around. Leveraging Big Data reduces your costs significantly in two major areas—storage and processing. In the other areas, the differences are less substantial. Before we develop a comprehensive framework to capture the total cost of Big Data initiatives in your organization, let's start with a simpler discussion around the various spend categories in Big Data:

> ➤ Procurement of or instrumentation for data collection (can be substantial on a case-by-case basis)

> ➤ Hardware investments or rental costs for storage and processing of data (usually much less when compared to traditional technology approach)

> ➤ Software licenses to build and run your environment (a lot of which is available freely)

> ➤ People-related costs for those engaged in analytics, development, and maintenance of the ecosystem (usually, a small number of very specialized resources)

> ➤ Physical infrastructure and general administrative costs (usually not different from any other project or initiative of a team of similar size)

In the next five sections, we will discuss some specific nuances of these various types of costs.

Data collection costs

If your organization already has a lot of data and your Big Data project(s) are geared towards using the existing and normally incoming data, you do not have to worry about data collection costs; they are already included in the normal operations of your company. Otherwise, this might become a big contributor to the total cost of your Big Data initiative.

Depending on what you are trying to achieve using Big Data, you need to first decide what additional data you need and how you will get it. If you are trying to capture operational information of some ecosystem or machines, you will most likely have to install sensors to get that data. This will lead to many different cost items, which are as follows:

> ➤ Physical sensor cost
>
> ➤ Installation costs of sensors
>
> ➤ Possible local aggregation or temporary storage of the raw sensor data
>
> ➤ Transmission costs from collection points to your Big Data storage location
>
> ➤ Maintenance of the collection infrastructure
>
> ➤ Other cost items that might be unique to your situation

If you are trying to build analytics and business models on data that somebody is already collecting, you may need to buy that data; this will involve some cost. If you are already collecting data but have them stored in different locations and systems, plus some of the data is structured while some of it is unstructured, you will need to build new interface systems to get all of the data into your Big Data environment; you will need to consider the cost of building and maintaining these interfaces as part of your data collection costs.

Advancement in communication technologies is reducing the cost of data collection and transmission, but if you are trying to capture machine data from thousands of units spread across a large geographic region, this might still be a considerable portion of your spend in Big Data. In such cases, even if your project is in a pilot mode, try to negotiate long-term bulk contracts with sensor manufacturers, telecom providers, and other such ecosystem participants. Structure your contract in such a way that you have very low minimum commitment thresholds, and your price per unit of purchase comes down substantially as your volume grows.

Often, your analytics might be based on data to which you have easy access but might not technically own. For example, you have sold some machines to customers and want to do analytics on the performance data of those machines. Unless you have specifically claimed your rights to the data in your initial sale contract, in many countries, the law will deem the owner of the asset to be the owner of the data also.

In another example, as a consumer, you own your financial transaction data or your telecom usage data unless you have assigned the rights to the service provider. In all such situations, you may end up paying a considerable sum of money to the owner of the data once they start seeing the value of their data. So, we recommend that before you go too much further, ensure that you have legal rights to the data you are performing analytics on to avoid any future surprises.

Storage and processing costs

Data storage has become a big industry in its own right, worth over $70 billion. Companies are also spending a noticeable portion, anywhere between 12-15 percent, of their IT budget, on data storage alone. Matt Komorowski has done some interesting research on the cost of storage between 1980 and 2009. His analysis has revealed that in the past 30 years, space per unit cost has doubled roughly every 14 months. His data tells us that the hard disk cost to store a gigabyte of data has come down from around $200,000 to less than 10 cents in this period! In 1956, the first hard drive, RAMAC305, was introduced; it had a capacity of 5 megabytes, was of the size equivalent to two refrigerators, and bore a cost of $10,000 per megabyte of storage. Now, you can buy a storage device with one terabyte capacity for less than $1000, and it will fit into your pocket. This device can store more than 1,000,000 times the data as compared to the hard drive of 1956, for a fraction of the cost. There has been significant progress in the storage technologies that has brought down the cost.

In *Chapter 4*, while discussing the storage infrastructure, we have discussed the technology choices in this space in detail. When finally making your selection, you need to balance the raw storage capacity cost and processing power/speed of the infrastructure. Depending on your application, sometimes, you will have to tilt in favor of better processing capabilities even though it might be slightly more expensive. For example, if you are working on a trading platform or something that does analytics of credit card transactions for fraud detection, you need multilayer data communication and huge volumes of data transfer at very high velocity; in such a situation, you not only need lot of storage, but also need the ability to process data very quickly.

When dealing with Big Data, you also need to balance between total capacity and number of nodes for storage and processing. Based on your requirements, explore multiple options and select the most optimal one with easy future scalability.

Today, you have many choices to store and host your Big Data—you can build the infrastructure on-premises in your organization or use a cloud-based hosting service such as those provided by Amazon, Microsoft Azure, or countless other new players. There are two primary factors that you need to consider in deciding between the two options of storing internally or hosting externally on the cloud—cost of ownership and long-term maintenance ease. In both cases, you need to make your assessment on at least a 5-year horizon. If you are just starting off or are a part of a small business, you can start off with minimal investments in hardware infrastructure and hire some talent to manage the infrastructure.

Until companies establish their long-term Big Data strategy and roadmap, we have seen that most of them take this approach towards infrastructure. Building your own infrastructure allows you to understand the storage and processing environment better, but if you do not have the right expertise in your business, it might increase the learning time.

Software licensing costs

Big Data technologies emerged and evolved in the open source era. Consequently, most of the capabilities to leverage Big Data are available freely in the open source world, where there is no technology licensing cost. In fact, you can build a complete Big Data environment without spending a single dollar on any licensing. In the last few years, large technology vendors such as EMC, Oracle, IBM, SAS, Cloudera, and others have come up with licensed solutions that address many aspects of the Big Data architecture. Some of them offer freeware with basic capabilities and licensed software with more advanced capabilities. Currently, there is no single provider of a single packaged solution that covers the entire gamut of Big Data technologies; it might be some time before anything like that happens.

There are pros and cons of using freeware versus licensed software. If you are using freely available tools and code, you may need more programming and analytical expertise to make use of them for your specific needs. Some of the licensed software solutions offer improved data-management capabilities in terms of indexing, metadata definitions, performance optimization, and security.

We would recommend a hybrid environment to use freeware and licensed software. For areas that anyway require extensive programming such as modelling and analytics, if you have the people who can perform those tasks, do not buy packaged software. These considerations will also have to be framed in the context of your organizational policies such as usage of non-verified freeware, maintenance standards, and so on. If you are at the beginning of your journey, try to use more of freeware and programming rather than investing in expensive software.

People costs

One of the biggest expenses in any Big Data project is the cost of people involved in the project. In the previous chapter, we discussed the unique skill sets of data scientists, experimental analysts, application developers, infrastructure specialists, change leaders, and project managers required to deliver your Big Data objectives. Most of these skills are rare and therefore expensive. For a comparable data warehouse or business intelligence type of project, this is one area where you might end up spending more in the Big Data world. Sometimes, repeated unstructured analysis and extensive data maintenance activities might involve more human effort, which could escalate your costs. Keep this in view as you progress in your journey.

To keep costs in check, try and use your extended ecosystem as much as possible. Leverage academics for data science activities. Use graduate students or freelance consultants for programming; these are good strategies to get started. You benefit from their past and vast experience and also might be able to contain costs.

However, our recommendation is that you should not compromise in this spend category. To gain traction across your organization and to realize the desired business benefits, it is critical to have the right people on board.

Infrastructure and administrative costs

Usually, infrastructure and administrative activities do not become burdensome in Big Data projects, but you need to capture them accurately to get a sense of the total cost of ownership for the initiative. In infrastructure, your main expenses will be towards physical data's center space, cooling, power, and maintenance. Depending on how much data you end up storing and what strategy you undertake between hosting internally or externally on the cloud, these costs could start becoming bigger. Administrative costs are also minimal and typically include normal ones in any project.

However, if your initiative leads to extensive change in your business processes or operating rhythm, you need to include change management costs as well. If this becomes a sizeable portion of your investment consideration, call it out separately instead of bundling in this category.

Maintenance costs

Maintenance also spans across most of the other categories. We are calling it out separately here because some companies prefer to bucket them differently for financial reporting reasons. If you do not want to include it as a separate category (represented vertically in the following context diagram), you can also represent it horizontally.

In maintenance, you should include any hardware or software upgrades, people dedicated only for maintenance activities, replacement of data collection instrumentation (if any), and other such activities. As your data volume will be growing over time, even for the same project, you will incur expenses for additional hardware and query development/ maintenance. You can either include this in their respective categories or under maintenance; if you choose the latter, then make maintenance a horizontal phase rather than a vertical category.

Capturing the costs

In capturing the costs, you should represent the costs for individual projects. If you have multiple projects running, figure out a way to judiciously apportion the total cost between the different projects based on the physical or human resources they actually use. Sometimes, you will not be able to fully use all the people and computing infrastructure that you have; in such cases, you can capture the related costs of the unused capacity of people and computing infrastructure at the enterprise level. This will allow you to determine the true cost and benefit of individual projects and also for the overall Big Data initiative.

Cost Context Framework

Now, let's take these cost categories and create a context diagram against the various key activity groups of a Big Data project. This will help us develop a perspective of how much you are spending to accomplish what objectives:

	Instrumentation	Hardware	Software	Development	Infrastructure & Administrative	Maintenance
Collection						
Storage						
Processing						
Modeling						
Analysis						
Publishing						

This context diagram will be immensely useful if you are ever asked by your management or finance leadership to provide a comparison with traditional technologies. Many of these cells will be empty; for example, you are unlikely to have any instrumentation costs for anything other than data collection. At the outset, while you are preparing your budget, fill in this table to create the baseline context diagram. Periodically update this table and compare how the costs are progressing.

Monetizing your Big Data

There is no argument that Big Data creates tremendous value in real money. Monetizing this value helps in many ways:

➤ Creates other potential sources of revenue for your business

➤ Develops better appreciation around Big Data in your organization

➤ Helps better manage your Big Data investments

➤ Establishes a deeper sense of ownership in your Big Data team

Earlier in the chapter, when we discussed valuation, we only considered the benefits to the business. Subsequently, we looked at the investments involved with realizing those benefits using Big Data. *When you are pursuing monetization, you need to subtract the costs from benefits to understand the true value of data.* So, in the remainder of this section, when we talk about value, we are referring to the net impact value.

There are many ways you can monetize Big Data; we will discuss three of them in this section:

➤ Direct business impact

➤ Selling data externally

➤ Valuation of Big Data

Direct business impact

Direct business impact is the most implemented method for valuation of data. You will often see companies, analysts, or researchers talking about how Big Data has added value. One example is how Walmart added over a billion dollars annually in additional sales using data and analytics. In a previous section of this chapter, where we focused on capturing the value of data, we discussed the process of calculating direct business impact. The sponsoring executives and shareholders of your business will be very keen to understand this value. While following this method, our recommendation is that you capture only the current value of your data and analytics. The key, as we discussed earlier, is to have an established process to define and capture the impact and value of the impact in a systematic and sustained manner. It will be good to separately show the primary, secondary, and potential value of data as you keep building your Big Data program.

Selling data externally

Companies have been selling and buying data for a very long time. Telephone companies sell their subscriber data to all sorts of businesses that are interested in reaching out to you to promote their goods and services (I'm sure you know all about those pesky telemarketing calls). Internet service providers and popular websites are also doing similar things. Utilities providers also sell their consumer and consumption data to interested parties. Energy usage data is very useful for companies that sell to or service facilities. If you are an OEM or a service provider to facilities, you can, in turn, sell detailed usage data with appropriate details to utility companies to help them get a better understanding of usage patterns and design better demand-management policies. Many research companies have major businesses based around buying and selling data and insights. Governments collect a lot of data; in some countries, they are opening up a lot of non-sensitive and non-personal data to general public and corporate entities to use.

Big Data helps store and process *all* data inexpensively, so we expect data transactions to increase in the near future. The key for you is to find a party that might be interested in your data. They will use this data to create new business models in areas you are currently not exploring or for research purposes. Most likely, they will enrich your data with input from other sources.

When selling your data to a third party, you need to be careful about three things:

> ➤ You own the data and have the rights to sell it
>
> ➤ The data you are selling will not create a competitive disadvantage for you, even though today a competitor may not be a recipient of your data
>
> ➤ There are no regulatory restrictions to your trading in data

Instead of an outright sale of data, you could also explore licensing options if your buyer wants access to the data for a period of time.

There are some other approaches as well. Recently, there have been some experiments with crowdsourcing ideas using data. You can work with another partner to develop business models and opportunities and share the fruits of such efforts. Crowdsourcing is increasingly becoming popular in many walks of life and commerce, so you need to carefully consider this option if you have limited resources or ideas.

Make a note

In his acclaimed book, Crowdsourcing, Darren Brabham presents many scenarios for the application of crowdsourcing in different walks of life. The public domain website, `www.crowdsourcing.org`, is another good source of information on this topic.

If you are a small business sitting on a lot of data, this route of creating commercial value out of data can be a very attractive opportunity for you to generate some extra cash, which you can invest back in your growth.

Valuation of Big Data

On the one hand, current accounting standards do not explicitly prevent you from taking the value of data into your company's balance sheet and books. On the other hand, there are no clear standards to do so either. In fact, the topic of creating book value of data is quite ambiguous and subject to different interpretations by different auditors and authorities. Most legal and accounting systems expect businesses to use the data to generate new revenue or new profits or both and take the impact of that in the books. This is considered a cleaner and safer approach.

A more common approach is for companies to pursue the path of creating perceived value of data. Investors and stock markets can be persuaded to pay a premium for this perceived value of data even though it may not reflect on the books of the company. There are techniques to assess value of intellectual property such as patents, but the same cannot be applied as it is in the case of data. Patents directly lead to sources of revenue, whereas data leads to insights, which in turn might lead to sources of revenue and/or profits; this makes the path a bit convoluted.

To create a perceived value of Big Data, you start by calculating the direct business impact as a result of data and analytics. In the direct impact, while you have considered the current or near term value, in this method, you need to look at your future value and potential value of data as well. If you can prove a sustained growing impact on the business, that is, if you can establish appreciation in the value of data over a period of time, you can even use a multiplier to determine the final value. This is similar to when investors are willing to pay a multiplier on your net earnings or for the goodwill and brand value of your company.

If you choose to embark on the path of formal valuation of your data, we have a few suggestions:

- ➤ Be conservative when you assign financial value to data
- ➤ Even though you may start your value identification and assignment process from an individual initiative, consider the entire volume across your enterprise to assign value to any data
- ➤ Have irrefutable proof of the monetary value your business has been able to accrue as a result of data and analytics; this means that you need to have clearly captured the pre- and post- scenarios with relation financial performance
- ➤ Get your finance organization to sign off on your calculations
- ➤ Check with your legal department whether you have data ownership issues to be able to claim value for it
- ➤ Perform external validation of your data valuation methodologies and actual data valuation using other data scientists, actuaries, and auditors

You should perform this type of valuation if you are planning for an extraordinary event such as major external capital infusion, public offering, divesture, or acquisition. Your investors and stakeholders will expect you to have this type of valuation ready because data as an asset is an important for them.

Managing your Big Data investments

One of the best ways to capitalize on the uniqueness of Big Data is to manage investments as if you are doing so for a hedge fund. Using this approach gives you lot of flexibility over normal investment management techniques followed in corporations, and these flexibilities will help address the evolving and unique nature of Big Data:

- ➤ Normal micro level monitoring and governance processes around technology investments can be modified
- ➤ You can start or stop the investments at any point
- ➤ Choose where to invest, and you might not have to justify your choices to the rest of the company
- ➤ Track the returns of each project, but retain the flexibility to report and justify returns for the entire portfolio, allowing you to experiment a bit
- ➤ Reinvest the returns into more Big Data initiatives to generate more value

Just as hedge funds employ four key investment strategies (global macro, directional, event-driven, and relative value), similarly, you can classify your Big Data investments as follows:

- ➤ Addressing enterprise needs (global)
- ➤ Improving organizational performance in specific areas that show trends of promise or problems (directional)

➤ Addressing some unique business problems that have cropped up (event-driven)

➤ Exploring how to take advantage of areas where organizational performance is below internal or industry benchmarks (relative value)

This provides an easy-to-understand and easy-to-communicate framework to classify your Big Data initiatives and justify investments.

Just as a hedge fund manager will try to diversify their portfolio, you should also try to apply Big Data in different aspects of your business to explore the possibilities. However, as you will be managing a portfolio instead of every project, you can apply some arbitrage between the projects towards expectations of returns or time when the returns are expected.

Whether you choose to take the hedge fund approach or stick to your normal organizational practices, you should always measure the return on investment (ROI) for each project as well as calculate the return on net assets (RONA) for your entire Big Data portfolio. While ROI helps you understand the benefits of individual projects, RONA helps you assess the financial performance of Big Data investments in totality.

The formulas to calculate ROI and RONA are very simple and standard across the world:

➤ ROI = (Gains from Investment – Investment) / Investment

➤ RONA = Net Income / (Fixed Assets + Net Working Capital)

Notes for financial performance calculations:

➤ Investment should include all the expenses we discussed in the preceding section

➤ Net income should be the residual value of the benefits after you have deducted the investments

➤ Fixed assets should include all your capitalized hardware and software investments

➤ Net working capital should include your operating cost of the Big Data environment without considering any new projects

Ideally, you should not consider the monetized value of your Big Data as a fixed asset. If you are selling data, you should include that in your income.

Your ROI should be definitely more than the standard cost of capital value used by your organization, and your RONA should be higher than the organizational RONA goals.

Ideally, you should prepare and publish a balance sheet of your Big Data investments to your management and other key stakeholders. You can take the relevant sections of a normal balance sheet and build one up for your Big Data world.

Summary

In 1992, in the Wall Street Journal, the great management guru Peter Drucker said, "From being organized around the flow of things and the flow of money, the economy is being organized around the flow of information". Today, nothing can be closer to the truth than this prophecy.

This was a crucial chapter for us to understand the financial aspects of Big Data. We learnt about how Big Data creates value in the near term and in the longer term through the business benefits it brings to bear. Big Data is less expensive, not free. Many people have the misconception that by putting in a Hadoop cluster, they have started leveraging Big Data. However, there are many other aspects to it; we learnt about many of them and how they impact Big Data projects monetarily. We touched upon a key topic of creating a context diagram to understand, analyze, and visualize Big Data costs with respect to the various aspects and phases of a project. Finally, we worked on ideas that lead to monetization of the Big Data ecosystem.

You have previously learned how to use Big Data to differentiate and win in the marketplace; in this chapter you learned about techniques on how to make money using Big Data and how to articulate and optimize the spend.

In the next chapter, we will start building the very important change management framework to drive the sustainability of the gains of Big Data for your business. We will once again build a framework to simplify driving a difficult change management exercise.

7

Driving Change Effectively

With the advent of Big Data, the world has been changing over the past few years. In the preceding chapters, we discussed many of these changes and how to integrate them into your current organizational fabric. We talked about how companies can make sense of huge volume, velocity, variety, variability, and veracity of data and effectively visualize the analytics derived from this data. New organizational strategies and business models are being enabled by Big Data. Many management practices and beliefs are getting challenged.

Often, organizations make the mistake of considering Big Data a technology problem; technology here is a mere enabler. Embracing the true power of Big Data requires organizations to adapt to different thinking and behavior. Effective change management becomes crucial in such an environment. You need to transition your people and teams to the future state of business enabled by Big Data. In his HBR Blog on **Predicting Customer's Behavior**, Alex Pentland made a profound observation, "Behavior is largely determined by social context." He further goes on to say in the same article that "Markets are not just about rules or algorithms; they are about people and algorithms together."

Big Data can give insights into what to change; it is up to the people in your business to actually change something.

Change management deals with taking individuals or groups of people into a future state. The Change Management Learning Center (www.change-management.com) defines change management as the application of a set of tools, processes, skills, and principles to manage the people's side of the change to achieve the required outcomes of a project or initiative. In his July 2011 interview with Forbes, Dr. John Kotter describes minimizing the distractions and impacts of the change as a primary goal of change management.

Change management as a formal discipline of study and practice is only a few decades old. In the early 1960s, some management thinkers started discussing change management concepts, best practices, and significance for sustainable business impact. Julien Phillips from McKinsey is rumored to have published the first change management model in 1982 in the Human Resource Management journal. Since then, a lot has been written and talked about for effective change management. Even industry- and context-specific models have been developed. In the area of Big Data, there is no established change management framework, but the topic is of highest significance because of the quantum, depth, and breadth of changes and their impact. In this chapter, you will understand how to put in context the changes ushered by Big Data for your organization and we will then equip you with a framework to manage the change process.

Understanding changes caused by Big Data

Leading Big Data thinkers such as Prof. Mayer Schoenberger, Alex Pentland, and others have been educating the world about some of the fundamental changes being caused by Big Data. The seven key ones are described in the following sections.

Correlation is leading to valuable insights without having to wait for specific causal analysis

Fast and effective processing of lot of data can now accurately predict what is going to happen next without understanding deeply why it is happening. So, the value of evolving data is taking precedence over static knowledge acquired through lot of hard work, perseverance, and significant investment in developmental programs. Prof. Mayer-Schoenberger remarks, "Correlations let us analyze phenomenon not by shedding light on its inner workings but by identifying a useful proxy for it."

This change requires organizations to develop new skills and archive some of the old competencies. For example, in earlier times, retail companies used to employ armies of market research analysts who used to go door to door or talk to hundreds and thousands of customers; now, these companies rely more on statisticians and behavioral scientists. Decision-making processes that previously relied on the knowledge and understanding possessed by groups or individuals who could help with causality analysis (answering the why) are now going to also rely on possible outcome scenarios that the data is predicting. The shift can create instability and insecurity in groups or people that were previously considered the custodians of formal and tribal organizational or business knowledge. The shift is also equally critical for executives who have to use their gut feeling less in a decision-making process.

Being able to identify patterns and possibilities has become more important than being 100 percent accurate

The previous preoccupation with causality and limited data required data to be pristine so that the analysis could be accurate. With Big Data, there is lot of data to deal with, and the pursuit of perfection becomes very challenging. Since Big Data deals more with probabilities, the intensity for perfection is less. So now, decision making has to be based more on patterns and possibilities rather than being exact. Prof Mayer-Schoenberger tells us that what we lose in accuracy at the micro level is made up in deeper and quicker insights into the macro environment.

This necessitates more risk-taking abilities in decision makers; this also requires such people to have a deeper understanding of their business and operating environment, while having strong capabilities to simulate various scenarios so that risks can be properly addressed. Managers working with Big Data need to have higher tolerance for experimentation as opposed to living in a prescriptive and definitive world. More agility is required in decision-making managers to adapt quickly as data keeps bringing new insights. At the same time, these managers need to have a strong compass on what they have set out to achieve, as their goals need to have a general sense of direction.

Managerial practices will be more influenced by inductive thinking

In the absence of the ability to process a lot of data and do it fast, traditional decision making relied more on past experiences, knowledge, and deductive thinking. Generally, you start with a broad level hypothesis, then validate it, or otherwise, by applying data-based testing. Inductive reasoning, on the other hand, starts with observing and analyzing the data, identifying patterns, and then crafting a hypothesis. Since Big Data makes storage and processing of huge volumes and variety of data easier, we can now recourse to more inductive thinking. This shift requires managers to rely less on their intuition and past experiences and depend more on data and insights from it.

Analytics can now be based on streaming data or static data or a combination of both

Before Big Data started becoming popular, a lot of data was not used in organizations because it was very difficult to deal with. Static data captured in notes and other unstructured formats was used as a reference point at best, if at all, while any analysis was performed. The effort and cost of poring over unstructured data was huge due to technology limitations. It was often relegated as being subjective and unreliable, thereby unusable for meaningful analysis. Streaming data was similarly difficult to capture and make sense of, so it was discarded as well.

Big Data is changing all of that. Usually, the volume and richness of the unstructured and streaming data outshines the structured data for most businesses. For companies invested in Big Data technologies, any significant analysis now includes structured and streaming data along with the easy to deal with structured data.

For example, to decide an employee's performance, line managers and human resources departments relied primarily on structured formal performance evaluation processes and data capturing. The highest frequency of these events is never more than once a quarter. On the other hand, employees are interacting with other employees and customers every day; they are completing tasks and projects weekly or monthly; every day they are performing something that can be captured from their work output, corporate social media interactions, e-mails, and other sources. Now, technology allows us to make sense of these unstructured and streaming data points in our consideration of performance of the employee.

Normalization of data is no longer a prerequisite for analytics to function effectively

Earlier, technology choices required data to have the same semantics to be able to analyze it on a common platform. Semantics in this discussion includes format, syntax, etymology and lexicology, among other properties of data. The variety of sources and context of data required considerable efforts for normalization of data so that semantic remediation could be performed easily. Therefore, most of the analytics were oriented towards structured data from similar sources. Big Data allows us to deal with the messiness and variety of data so normalization is no longer such a big deal.

With reduced focus on normalization, managers and technology experts now need to broaden the scope of their data consideration. This requires them to have a much deeper and detailed understanding of the business and operational processes; basically, they need to understand every process in your business that generates some form of data. They not only need to understand the process but also how data gets created in that process and what it might mean or the interpretations it can lead to. Therefore, managers and learning development organizations have to plan for a broader understanding of the business for people who will be involved with or impacted by Big Data projects.

Data in itself is becoming an asset

We discussed this phenomenon extensively in the previous chapter. Previously we could afford to be less sensitive about data, but since data is acquiring such unprecedented value, we need to more organizational education the significance of data and its vulnerabilities.

Paradigms around risks and ethics are changing dramatically

Big Data enables data democracy, but at the same time, normal rules around privacy and anonymity are exposed to getting challenged. Increasingly, the lines between data and analytics will also get blurred. This leads to people being concerned about their personal and business data being exposed to others; at the same time, barriers to collecting the same data have also reduced, so there is not a whole lot that individuals and businesses can do. This leads to the dark side of Big Data.

Big Data technologies are also reducing the necessity and influence of human effort, intuition, and intervention to reach a conclusion. Additionally, data does not take into account intention, so conclusions about human action can be divorced from their intent. Some some people might develop a tendency to shirk their individual accountability for decisions and actions, and blame everything on data.

Make a note

Big Data is not exact, and there will always be a human element in any decision-making process.

These are very contentious and difficult problems to deal with for organizations. Businesses will now have to develop deep thinking and robust processes to address the following aspects:

➤ Data ownership and privacy concerns among employees and customers

➤ Guidelines on how to share personal and business information on social media and other such data outlets

➤ Personal accountability for decisions and actions even if they are taken with the help of data and analytics

➤ The organization does not become completely fixated with data and starts an era of data dictatorship

Kord Davis, formerly a consultant with Capgemini, has suggested a good framework to understand and manage risks and ethics in his book *Ethics of Big Data: Balancing Risk and Innovation*. The framework suggested is useful in a corporate environment, and you need to have basic understanding of Big Data to make use of this book.

The significance of changes

Failing to manage the changes effectively will either put organizations at risk because traditional competition, adjacent players, or nontraditional competitors who use Big Data more effectively can put the organizations' business model and long-term viability at risk.

One interesting example in this context is how online advertising is changing. When online advertising was first introduced, online platforms used to push content based on some prearrangements with sponsor companies. So, all of us visiting a particular site at a particular time would get to see the same advertisement. The ad space would be auctioned or sold in a bulk or spot deal, which used to be predetermined for time, duration, and money. Leading edge companies in this space take a very different approach now. As soon as they see a user loading a page, they do real-time analytics on the user profile, reference it to past activity, and create preference profiles. On a real-time basis, they auction these preferences for ad push to sponsor content providers or brokers. The participants respond to the auctions. The successful bidder's advertisements are shown by the time the user has loaded the page, all happening in less than a second. So now, you and I will see different ads while visiting the same site at the same time. As a corollary, you will also see similar themed ads running while you are visiting different websites. In fact, for the past several months since I have been working on this book, every time I go to the Internet even to news sites, I always see a Big Data ad! There are very sophisticated Big Data engines running in the background that are making sense of all this streaming data on a real-time basis and deciding which advertisements users might be interested in.

In this example, there are four changes that Big Data has introduced:

> New business models around dynamic real-time auctions

> Incentive models for participants in the process

> Operating processes required by companies auctioning the ad slot and those responding to the auction

> Skills required for analysis and response

Our experience and research demonstrates that Big Data always brings changes in the context of the preceding four dimensions.

Previously, such decisions were made by people who were considered gurus who understand consumer behaviors, trends, and user preferences. So now we need new skills around analytics and also need to use people with legacy skills around understanding consumer behaviors in a different way. Changes brought by technology are often rapid. Changes brought by Big Data, when it gets more momentum in mainstream businesses, will bring changes at a lightning speed.

Changes have to be identified and dealt with in the context of business models, people, organization structures, and operating processes with respect to skills and incentives.

Applying the IMMERSE framework to manage change

Now, you have a good understanding of most of the changes in your world that Big Data is causing. Right away, the question is how do you take all of these changes and manage them for your business. There are many change-management methodologies and frameworks that you can adopt as well. Holger Nauheimer, a famed change management consultant and author, has created a collection of tools, methodologies, and strategies for change management titled *The Change Management Toolbook*, which is actually available for free download.

We have not found any specific ones developed for Big Data initiatives. We will now introduce a framework called IMMERSE to help you manage the changes. IMMERSE stands for **Identify, Modulate, Mitigate, Role play, Educate, Show,** and finally **Effect**; we believe these are the various stages an individual or a team has to go through in the change process. This framework is a progressive sequential one, which you should run in iterations to improve and make themsustainable. The following diagram presents a summarized view of how this process works.

Remember that managing change is a process not an event. To make it effective, you start at one point and keep improvising as you go along, based on the feedback and effectiveness experienced.

Identify

The first step in this process is to identify the changes. You need to ascertain the changes that are happening at the industry level, what your competition is doing, and what is altering within your business. As mentioned earlier, the changes have to be identified in the context of business models, operating processes, organization structures, individual roles and responsibilities, and incentive models in the industry and for your people.

Some of the key questions you need to ask at this stage are:

How is the industry changing?

Here, you need to reflect on the changing business models, trends, products and services, customer expectations and engagement, and convergence or divergences with other industries. You need to paint a macro picture that will build a compass or baseline for consideration and help you deep dive into the other questions.

What are the competitive actions? How are existing players responding to the changing business models and operating processes?

You should find out what your traditional competitors are doing to take advantage of data and analytics. You need to research how the existing players are responding to the changing business models and operating processes. It is difficult to do so but immensely useful if you can find out the reasons behind their particular action or approach. To get this information, you could:

> ➤ Start with annual and quarterly reports of the company along with the corresponding analyst briefings
>
> ➤ Check out on the Internet what employees of the organization are publishing on
>
> ➤ Listen to what people from these companies are presenting in the different industry conferences and forums
>
> ➤ Browse through social media for relevant forums to see what kind of discussions the employees of those organizations are engaging in
>
> ➤ Talk to people in the company without violating any confidentiality
>
> ➤ Talk to the industry influencers; they seem to know everything going on everywhere!

Who are the emerging new players?

Once you have completed the analysis for your existing competitors, scan the horizon for who are potentially going to pose competitive threats for you in future. They can be small niche players today with dreams of getting bigger tomorrow; they can be adjacent players in your industry; they can even belong to completely nonrelated industries from the current context. If your business belongs to one of these categories, think about the traditional players. Build and run with as many scenarios as you possibly can; ultimately, only the paranoid survive.

How are the industry economics getting impacted?

Think carefully about how data and analytics are changing how companies make money in your industry. Here, you also need to think about new incentive models getting introduced for the ecosystem participants. You need to ask questions like do your customers expect you to incentivize them to acquire data, and are there ways you can pay for the data and connectivity infrastructure through the value of analytics; make all such enquiries now. As you do this, go back and check whether you have incorporated these considerations in your value and benefits' calculations discussed in the previous chapter.

What are the possible impact areas for your business?

Big Data may not be affecting all parts of your business now; you need to know which the most impacted ones are. This will help you focus your energies on a more manageable effort. Do not worry about pin-pointing the impact level yet; we will tackle this in the next step. Presently, you need to have an exhaustive understanding of all the aspects of your business that are getting impacted significantly.

Modulate

Next, you need to get more specific in simulating how the changes are going to impact your business. In doing so, you need to answer a few questions:

What is the urgency for you to change?

You need to understand for how long you can continue to sustain and/or grow by remaining immune to these changes. Typically, if you have a very large business or are in a very niche market with strong demand, you will get a longer leash without changing, but for sure, you will be impacted—later if not sooner. You need to understand the timing so that you can plan and deploy your change actions accordingly.

How do your core competencies and key differentiators get impacted by this changing ecosystem?

Every successful organization has some core competencies that are difficult for others to emulate; you also have some. Similarly, every successful business will also have some strong differentiators that attract customers to them. You need to take stock of these core competencies and differentiators and simulate where they will stand with all the changes being introduced by Big Data.

What are the financial implications of your identified impact areas?

In the previous stage, you identified the impact areas. Now, put a number to those. You should consider revenue, profit, and market share impact, all of them in this calculation.

What are the foreseeable risks if you change?

If your business is working very well, you and your superiors might be averse to change unless there is a compelling reason. Usually, the perceived risks of introducing abrupt or disruptive changes reduce the propensity for change. So, you need to understand and modulate these scenarios well.

What are your organizational reserves to deal with the change?

You must know your bandwidth to accommodate the fallout of any change or decision not to change. In doing so, you need to consider financial reserves as well as your talent availability. You should ponder how much money and manpower you have to withstand the changing ecosystem.

Mitigate

In the third step, you determine your mitigation strategies for all the perceived risks. Once you know the business areas and threats posed by Big Data for those business areas, you contemplate making changes in the following aspects of your business:

What are the required business model changes?

In the business model, you need to primarily focus on how your business makes money and how it engages with customers and suppliers to do so. All your revenue generation streams and steps should be part of this study. This will include the different products and services you offer to your customers, how they perceive value in them, and how they are priced and delivered to customers.

What are the required operating model changes?

In an operating model, you look at the product or service-delivery food chain. You should account for all internal processes and activities involved that lead to your engagement with the customer. You must take into account the various departments and functions in your business that are involved in these processes. Normally, each process or activity will have some outcome metrics; you need to reflect on whether any of these are changing, and if so, what the new metrics and their threshold values are.

What are the organizational structure changes?

Now, you plot the impact of Big Data interventions on your current organization structure and how it needs to change to absorb the impact. Often, you will create new roles and functions while making some of the old ones redundant as necessitated by your business model or operating model changes. In an organization structure, you also need to consider the flow of information between various parts and layers of the organization. Before you think of the changes, it is recommended that you start with a clean slate, keeping only the customer and your end objectives in mind. Then, overlay your current organization on that model to understand the required changes. This approach is useful to limit the influences of current inefficiencies.

What new skills do you need to imbibe in your people?

Once you know the model and structure changes, translate these into what people need to do differently now. This will lead you to the new skills and behavioral competencies required in your employees. You need to assess the gaps you can cover through training and the skills you need to acquire afresh. Sometimes, doing a comprehensive skill inventory at this stage is useful because you may uncover some skills and talent existing in your business that might actually help you further a Big Data program.

How do you excite people with new incentive models?

Ecosystem players in your business, especially your employees and suppliers (if you have any), understand how you value their performance and contribution through the compensation and incentive models you have in place. If you are requiring them to change their current behavior and actions, you need to tweak your compensation and incentive programs to reflect that.

Educate

Once you have identified the changes, understood their impact, and created a plan to ready your business for the amended ecosystem, you need to develop a communication and training package to help your employees understand the changes. We will discuss more on the development of this package in the next chapter. Once it is ready, you also need to create a mechanism to capture how the education process is working. Some of the key things you need to cover in the educate stage are:

What is Big Data and how is it impacting the world?

Define Big Data, share examples of Big Data from real world, and discuss a few examples of new businesses or business models that have been made possible by Big Data. This is an introductory session, so keep it the least technical as possible. Use examples from everyday life and your business world to help people put a context to what you are saying.

How can data sciences and advanced analytics help businesses?

Use examples from different industries to demonstrate how different companies created new customers or created new value for existing customers and increased their business or increased their competitiveness.

What are the changes in your industry driven by Big Data?

If you have examples of Big Data being applied in your industry, talk about them here. Definitely discuss the implications of Big Data for your industry—either in terms of business models, markets, or operating processes. It is important to help people paint a picture of what the industry is going to look like in future. If you foresee new competition, talk about them and their effect.

How is your company planning to respond to these changes?

Talk about the specific initiatives in your company to address these industry level changes. It would be great to showcase in the past how your business has a track record of mitigating external challenges. Reaffirm your confidence on the Big Data initiatives and explain to people how it is solving your challenges.

What impact do these changes have for the individual employees and the teams they belong to?

In a changing environment, people are most concerned about the impact on them. Here, you need to discuss the changes in organizational structures and operational processes mostly. Make the discussion as specific to your audience as possible. Transparency leads to comfort and employee alignment in these situations.

What new skills and competencies they need to learn to be more successful in the Big Data world, and how do they take advantage of data and analytics to perform better?

It is relatively easy for people to understand that change is impacting them, but rarely do they appreciate that they also need to change, learn new things, and use new tools. Use a lot of examples and specifics when talking about these topics. Make this more of a show-and-tell session rather than a presentation-loaded session.

What are the behavioral changes expected in the employees as a result of the Big Data initiatives?

It is not enough for people to learn new skills and use new tools to effectively use Big Data. Your employees will now need to think and behave differently as well. This is probably the most difficult part of the change management process, especially for people with a lot of legacy in your business. Explaining the rationale for behavior change and using examples will make the process effective. Try and get influencers and opinion-makers from among your employee base to be your advocates.

What will the company look like in future as a result of these Big Data initiatives?

Your employees will commit better to the change process if they see a bright future ahead; they tie their fortunes and well-being to those of your company. So, simulate the environment to show how Big Data is going to transform the company in future and what it will look like. Imagine a day in the life of your employees today; show a day in the life of a similar employee in future. Create similar examples with customers as the focal point. These will help drive the message.

Why is Big Data so crucial for your business?

For anything new being introduced, multiple reinforcements always help strengthen the assimilation process. Now, summarize all the benefits of Big Data for your business.

What are the consequences of not responding to the changes?

This step is to reinforce the urgency and criticality of Big Data for your business. In some of the earlier steps, you created a sense of excitement, a sense of accomplishment, a sense of security in your employees; now, do the reverse. These opposing emotions will drive the message hard.

Role play

To help people absorb the changes, we have seen that one of the most effective methods is to make employees do some role play simulations in the new changed world. This helps them internalize what has been shared during the educate phase and make it stick for a long time. There are many popular techniques for role playing—my personal favorite is War Games. You divide your team into groups and they go through three exercises:

> ➤ First, they think and behave like your customers to identify what some of the emerging expectations are that can be fulfilled using Big Data. It is important to develop examples of how their operations can be positively impacted using Big Data in your products and services.

> ➤ Next, they play the role of different competitors and create scenarios of how they will develop and implement strategies to win in the market place.

> ➤ Lastly make them apply Big Data to transform your business in responding to changing customer expectations and competitive actions.

This approach also helps your people to get a rounded perspective of the changing world. Ideally, these role play sessions should be held offsite so that the normal business environment does not influence their thinking, and neither are they distracted by the normal duties. Each role play session should last between 1-2 days. Depending on the quantum of changes, you may want to repeat these at some interval for better assimilation. Your change leader ideally should be able to play the role of a facilitator. However, get a professional facilitator if you need one and can afford one.

Show

This is a critical stage for you to convert the nonbelievers or difficult to change people in your organization. You can use the success stories from some pilot projects to do so. Even for the believers, you need to reinforce their faith; you need to help them improve their understanding. You start creating brand ambassadors for your Big Data initiative in the show stage. While doing your campaigns, please keep in mind a few key points:

> ➤ Talk about successes with tangible results

> ➤ Get the project team to interact with people if you can; get your customers to do this (even if internal) as well

> ➤ Talk to people about the future roadmap

> ➤ Create a simulated environment for future projects

> ➤ Contextualize the changes and benefits as it impacts the lives of your audience

> ➤ Create an opportunity for people to have follow-up conversations with you

Effect

The last stage is your realization phase where you implement the changes, capture the benefits, and keep adapting to sustain the benefits. Before you start in this phase, be clear to identify the key metrics you will use to measure and monitor success. Everybody involved with the initiative needs to be aligned on the definition and measurement methodologies for the metrics upfront to avoid any disappointment later. Your realization may extend for a long period of time, but do define a specific exit date for this phase. This will help you with proper project closure and handover to business as usual. You also need to set up the review schedule for the realization activities, and preferably also outline the agenda for the review sessions. Such a step will provide more predictability to this phase and ensure that people are committed to participate in the process.

Your typical effect stage will comprise three cyclical activities—**implement, review, and tweak**. You will implement the new business models, operating processes, and other changes first; then, after some passage of time, say every 3 months, review the impact of the changes on your performance metrics; then tweak either the analytics or the processes to get better results. If you see a sustained lack of success, do not be afraid to either scrap the project or make major course corrections.

Creating stakeholder groups to drive change

In your project team, you have a change leader. This person, as we have described in *Chapter 5, Building a Winning Team*, will act as your internal project team coach and also drive the entire change management program in your business. If the impact or span of the change is big, that is, if it crosses over multiple departments and involves hundreds of people, it will take more than a year to realize the benefits; we recommend that you create some stakeholder groups to make the change management more effective and pervasive.

We recommend that you do not create more than three such groups—a project group, work group, and review group.

Project group

This is your core project team comprising the various profiles we discussed in *Chapter 5, Building a Winning Team*. This team is primarily responsible for achieving the project objectives but should hand over the sustenance responsibilities to the work group.

Work group

The work group is the implementation team from your business, which will take forward the changes brought by Big Data. This is the team that will experience the output of Big Data efforts every day. The project team will focus on the technical aspects of the project, while the work group will focus more on the actual usage of the data and analytics on a regular basis. As part of the project, you may bring such people into your team, but they need to go back to the business once the project is over. You need to be clear up front on the division of roles and responsibilities along with the schedule for the project group and the work group.

Review group

This is the management group that is responsible for strategy, direction, monitoring, and facilitation. You should involve the person in charge of your business (it could be you), leaders of the various functional groups that support your business, and somebody from your business who can adequately represent the customer view. This team is different from your normal project-steering committees in that they are expected to have more involved participation rather than being a reporting and approving point.

We feel you should not call any of these committees because they come with such a bureaucratic connotation. Members of each group need to be personally accountable for the results of their teams and this should be included in their goal sheets.

Summary

In this chapter, we discussed the critical implications of having a robust change management plan for your Big Data initiatives because of the significant changes Big Data brings and the deep impact it creates on the business. The key changes we talked about are:

> ➤ How even without understanding the underlying reasons, it is now possible to predict outcomes by correlating data

> ➤ We do not need exact data to be able to predict future possibilities

> ➤ You can infer outcomes by looking at large volume of data, incidence of past events, and simulation of future scenarios

> ➤ You can analyze all kinds of data from all different sources at the same time without any inhibitions

> ➤ You do not have to be worried about normalizing data, that is, trying to define and interpret different types and sources of data from a common platform

> ➤ You have a very powerful asset in raw data

> ➤ You need deeper thinking about the risks and ethical issues with this massive data proliferation

We also understood that in most Big Data initiatives, there are often changes in:

➤ Business models

➤ Operating processes

➤ Organization structures

➤ People skills and behaviors

➤ Incentive models

To effectively manage the change process, we defined an iterative methodology called IMMERSE.

While we touched upon some aspects of developing communication plans as part of the change management process in this chapter, in the next one, we will delve deeper into how to effectively communicate across your organization about Big Data.

8

Driving Communication Effectively

Whenever there is a major project happening in your business, you will typically see one or a series of e-mails from your leaders, you might see a poster or two, a few trinkets or artifacts here and there, attend a few town-hall meetings, and read about it on your company's intranet. The primary purpose of all of these is to tell you and other employees about the project, get you engaged, and talk about the benefits of the project.

In the case of Big Data initiatives, you need to do more. There are three primary reasons for that:

This is a new subject and is heavily laced with technology and advanced statistics.

You want people to develop a better understanding so that they are adequately engaged and can apply the capabilities correctly. Otherwise, like a lot of other technology initiatives, many of the new capabilities will get developed but adapting those capabilities will be difficult after the initial euphoria. In this process, you might miss out on the desired competitive advantage.

Let's take an example from Enterprise Resource Planning (ERP) implementations. These projects are expected to streamline and automate a lot of your operational processes. Usually, these new ERP systems are expected to replace old legacy applications that serve individual operational processes. However, in several organizations, we see people who continue to use older legacy applications along with the new ERP systems; this happens because of peoples' familiarity with older systems and possibly some gaps in understanding how to use the new system.

Big Data usually involves lot of change management.

Compared to normal technology projects, Big Data initiatives usually bring more fundamental changes in how business is conducted. Time and again, people underestimate the quantum of changes in the operational process, business models, and skills. If people do not understand the depth and breadth of Big Data in relation to how your particular initiative(s) is going to change their lives, there's a possibility that you won't be able to achieve the goals of transformation you set out to undertake. For example, if you are streaming the operational and performance data from equipment to predict future problems, the technicians need to understand the process and rationale behind such predictions before they believe in them and act upon them. Also, it is quite likely that the outcome of your initiative will change with feedback in time to come; you need people to understand your initiative holistically so that they can give you the right feedback and adapt to future changes easily.

You want more ideas and initiatives; to pursue those, you need more evangelists.

American psychologist Rollo May once said, "Communication leads to community, that is, to understanding, intimacy, and mutual valuing". It is quite possible that you have a small business or a small team pursuing Big Data initiatives, and you want to build momentum around Big Data. To do that, you need the full force and participation of the entire organization behind you. So you need more people to understand the subject, what you are trying to do, and think about what more can be done.

You are at the last leg of your journey to make effective use of Big Data to transform and grow your business. Along with change management, which we delved into extensively in the previous chapter, communication is another extremely important but often ignored aspect to successfully leverage Big Data in your organization. Journalist Sydney J Harris once said, "The two words 'information' and 'communication' are often used interchangeably, but they signify quite different things. Information is giving out; communication is getting through". So we are dedicating an entire chapter to this topic.

Communication in this case goes beyond traditional channels and methods. Social media and the convergence of various communication channels, phenomenon that are being furthered by Big Data incidentally, have a significant influence on how people think and act. In this chapter, we will explore some best practices around successful sustained communication around Big Data.

Identifying your communication needs

The first step for you in identifying your communication needs is to recognize the various audience groups and the content you want to deliver to those groups. We feel you can divide your audience groups into three broad categories:

- Internal
- External
- Shareholder

The **Internal** group includes employees and contractors working in your organization, even those not belonging to your particular business unit. There are sections of this group that will be impacted more by your Big Data initiatives than others. We recommend that you consider everybody for your communication plan; if required, modulate the intensity and extent of your communication based on the impact levels. The **External** group includes customers; ecosystem partners in your business, such as suppliers; and business influencers—people such as analysts and consultants who can potentially sway your customers' opinion about your products and services. If your business has shareholders, we recommend that you classify them in a different group because while they are heavily invested in your business, they are not truly internal; also, their communication needs are different than those of the other two groups. If you have stock analysts or market analysts, that is, people who influence the valuation of your company, add them in the shareholder group; their expectations and outlook will be similar. In the next three sections, we will explore what you must include while communicating with these various audiences.

Communicating with the internal audience

This audience group needs the most extensive communication; they are the ones who carry your Big Data torch. Communication with this group needs to happen at least on three dimensions–overview, strategic cascade, and project communication.

Providing a general overview of Big Data

Since this is a new subject for most people, you will benefit in the long run by providing everybody in your organization with some information about what it is. In this overview, you need to include, at a minimum, the following topics:

- What is Big Data?
- What are some of the new technical capabilities that are transforming analytics? How are these impacting businesses?
- Why is your business so interested in Big Data? What are the threats and what are some of the near-term opportunities?
- How are you going about using Big Data in your business?
- How can people develop an appreciation for the value of data?

In the overview section, there are many deep technical and strategic topics that you are introducing to your internal teams, possibly exposing the concepts to many for the first time. So, you need to break down the concepts into descriptions that your audience can easily relate to. Use examples from your industry, business, and everyday life, to help people understand easily. For example, communicating the size of data is a very difficult task. Simply defining data size in terms of gigabytes or terabytes or petabytes makes little sense for most people. When we hear that Facebook has a billion members or that 400 million new tweets are created by active users everyday or that there are over 40 billion credit card transactions every year, we know that we are talking about big numbers and big data, but it is very hard for us to relate the magnitude. People know what data is, but cannot appreciate in physical terms what the size of it is. On the other hand, if you use the EMC infographic using the sand example shared at the beginning of this book, it presents a human face of Big Data that people might find easier to connect with. Keep the technical and business sophistication of your audience in mind when you develop the communication material.

Sharing the strategic cascade

In *Chapter 1, Building Your Strategy Framework*, we covered how to develop the strategic cascade quite extensively with examples. You need to share the strategic cascade with the entire organization; however, depending on the levels of the organization, you should emphasize some aspects of the cascade more. Use more supporting data to help people understand your strategic intent. As you go down in the organization, explaining the why and how becomes more important. You also need to clearly articulate the departmental, team, and individual goals to make the overall strategic goals a success. You need to relate capabilities that the people need to develop in the changing environment and specific actions or expectations from different roles and individuals in the context of the strategic cascade.

Communicating about Gold Coin projects

If you have adopted the Gold Coin approach, use the same model to communicate the project updates. Your Big Data aspirations will get delivered ultimately through the Gold Coins, so keeping everybody concerned in the loop about the project and its progress is crucial. There are many things about these Gold Coin projects you need to tell people, which are as follows:

> ➤ **Project overview**: What business problem is this particular project solving and how is it using data and analytics to solve this particular problem?

> ➤ **Schedule for the project**: What are the key milestones that different audience groups need to be cognizant of and when will the benefits impact them?

> ➤ **Team working on the project**: Who are the key players and why have they been chosen for this project?; this will increase the project's credibility.

> ➤ **Accomplishments**: Talk about all the major successes and new findings.

> ➤ **Lessons learned**: What are the things that we could improve in the way we are operating currently?

➤ **Changes**: You can relate to the five types of changes discussed in *Chapter 7, Driving Change Effectively.*

➤ **Available resources**: Training material, expert advice, knowledge artifacts, discussion forums, and so on.

Each Gold Coin project should have its own communication package, which should be updated with time. If you are also building a Gold Mine, as we discussed in *Chapter 2, Creating an Opportunity Landscape and Collecting Your Gold Coins*, share your thoughts and give people a glimpse of the future; their faith in your leadership and future orientation will increase. In all of this communication, ensure that you sanitize any content that might otherwise reveal your competitive differentiator.

Communicating with the external audience

There are at least three primary external stakeholders with different needs whom you need to reach out to with information on your Big Data initiatives.

Engaging with customers

You may need customers' permission to use some data that they might own. You may also want to establish your leadership position in the market by demonstrating your superior approach and services using data and analytics. So, sharing your Big Data initiatives with customers is very important. If you are only going to use the output of Big Data to push more services and products, you may want to temper down your communication. Nevertheless, it is a good idea to share and be transparent to avoid any future confusion. Customers will typically need to understand the initiatives, the benefits they will get out of them, and any financial- or service-level impact they might experience, and resolve if there are any lingering data ownership and privacy issues.

Swaying the business influencers

In many industries, there are groups of people including analysts and consultants who influence the buying preferences of your customers. In many cases, you may also encounter government or industry body regulators who can influence the trajectory of your business. Business influencers are all such people who can influence your market standing, branding, and acceptance. Sharing your Big Data initiatives can positively sway them to present your business in a favorable light to the market. Business influencers will typically need to understand how you are differentiating from competition using Big Data, what new products and services you are creating using Big Data, and how your customers are benefitting by your investments in Big Data. Regulatory entities will be very interested in your perspective on data security and ownership issues.

Roping in your ecosystem partners

Your ecosystem partners include all external stakeholders for your business who help you deliver. This includes your suppliers, consultants, and everybody else whose products and services you need in order to make your customers successful. Some of them may be impacted by your Big Data initiatives, while some others might be immune. However, it is important to enlist as many as possible in your Big Data journey once you are clear about your roadmap, because they could be a rich source of new ideas, resources, and collaboration, to make your Big Data plans successful. Engaging ecosystem partners also helps in furthering your branding and enticing new ones. These partners will normally like to understand what your Big Data play is, what you are specifically doing, what benefits they can get, and what is expected out of them. Their needs are somewhat similar to your internal employees' needs, but you need to curate the information being disseminated to them to protect your competitive and business edge.

Communicating with the shareholders

In most organizations, you are expected to be custodians for your shareholders—those who are funding your business and those who own your business. So, keeping them in the loop about your Big Data initiatives is important as they are the ultimate beneficiaries of your efforts. Your shareholders will normally be interested in four things about your Big Data initiatives:

> ➤ What are you doing?
> ➤ Why is it important?
> ➤ How are you creating value for them?
> ➤ What help, if any, do you need from them?

Their information needs will generally be less detailed compared to other audience groups. To get their attention and buy-in, you need to be very crisp in your communication and be very factual and value-oriented.

We discussed including stock analysts in this group earlier on. The level of detail you share with these value influencers might change, as shareholders have the right to know almost everything they ask about but stock analysts don't.

Once you have identified all your communication needs, list them down by audience group with as much detail as possible. This will be useful to identify common and targeted needs that can make your communication material development and messaging processes much easier. This will be required for your next step, which is developing the communication strategy.

Selecting your communication channels

Globalization and technology have made the commercial environment very complex and dynamic. This leads to a number of challenges for effective communication in the business world; some of the top ones are as follows:

> ➤ A lot of persistent information overload is happening at a rapid rate
> ➤ Attention spans are reducing drastically, and listening skills are eroding sometimes
> ➤ Too many distractions are increasing noise levels for people
> ➤ The lines between personal and professional communication are becoming blurred
> ➤ In-person interactions between employees are reducing, with an increasing reliance on technology
> ➤ A high convergence of different communication channels and methods is occurring
> ➤ Hierarchical management is being replaced by more participatory management
> ➤ Privacy and confidentiality of any communication has become more porous

Businesses today are expected to take quick and decisive actions in a dynamically changing and often globally integrated or influenced environment. Such decision-making can happen efficiently if the employees are properly educated and empowered. To effectively disseminate crucial pieces of communication around Big Data, it is critical to select the right channels to overcome the challenges we have discussed.

Communication channels

In today's technology-rich world, you have many choices from a plethora of communication channels. Let's now review some of the most common ones used by businesses across the world and understand their advantages and limitations:

Channel	Advantages	Limitations	Most suited audience groups
Company intranet	■ Wide reach ■ Standard messaging	■ Impersonal ■ One-way communication	People who are okay with generic information
Company social media	■ Can be targeted towards specific groups ■ Interactive ■ Appeals to younger employees	■ Can be difficult to moderate ■ May contain lot of noise communication ■ Not considered formal enough by some managers	Younger employees and those whose success depends on pervasive collaboration

Channel	Advantages	Limitations	Most suited audience groups
Public social media	■ Strong mass outreach ■ Good for image building	■ Porous ■ Unsuitable for company confidential information	People who have limited distance between personal and professional
Company newsletters	■ Wide reach	■ Impersonal one-way communication	All employees for information sharing
Town-hall meetings	■ Can be powerful if delivered by credible and powerful leaders	■ Ineffective for non-location-based employees	Office staff who need interaction and explanations
Small group meetings	■ Interactive nature ■ Ability to go into details and modulate conversations	■ Limited reach	People whose deep engagement is critical for the success of the initiative
Targeted e-mails	■ Focused ■ Able to get into details	■ Non-interactive	All who are impacted
Address by senior executives	■ Highly impactful if executives have a strong connect	■ Can expose vulnerabilities	All who are impacted
Posters and display boards	■ Great to generate interest and sublime messaging	■ Can be expensive	All

Channel	Advantages	Limitations	Most suited audience groups
Novelty items (articles such as t-shirts, mugs, mouse-pads, calendars, and so on)	■ Great to improve recall and excitement	■ Can be expensive depending on volume	Project team members
Quarterly reports / analyst briefings	■ Great forums for an external audience and market-oriented employees	■ Will cause strong tracking and follow-up on progress by external stakeholders and media	Shareholders and customers
Industry publications	■ Demonstration of thought leadership	■ Limited reach ■ Message complexity	Specialist audience
Newspapers and televisions	■ Mass reach ■ Can have strong brand impact	■ Very expensive	Mass external audience

Channel effectiveness

Communication starts with what you share, but gets complete with what the audience assimilates. So while the message has to be effective, the delivery channel also has to be equally effective for communication efforts to be successful. There are no golden rules for what method and which channel will work where. The decisions on methods and channels have to be made in the context of your business, people, objectives, and the current state. We recommend that you build a channel effectiveness matrix to take such decisions. When building this, you need to consider four aspect:

➤ **Audience group**: Which target groups you are trying to reach out to?

➤ **Reach**: How many people in a particular audience group use this channel?

➤ **Effectiveness**: How effective is the channel for this particular audience group?

➤ **Best-suited message type**: What kinds of messages are best delivered through this channel for the respective audience groups?

The following is an easy-to-use template for the same:

Channel	Audience Group	Reach	Effectiveness	Best-suited Message Type
Channel 1				
Channel 2				
Channel 3				
Example— Company intranet	Internal	90 percent of all employees	Medium— most people occasionally visit the intranet portal	Announcements and process details

While selecting your channels, also keep in mind the two Bs:

> ➤ **Bandwidth**: You may want to leverage all possible channels, but do you have enough people to help you drive the program across those channels? Digital platforms are effective and inexpensive but require lot of time, investment, and careful attention.

> ➤ **Budget**: How much money do you have to spend on the various channels?

Armed with the necessary knowledge and selection of your communication channels, you are now ready to work on building the communication strategy.

Building your communication strategy

Effective communication requires a potent strategy. Your communication strategy is built from many considerations:

> ➤ **Your goals and objectives**: You have already worked on them in *Chapter 1, Building Your Strategy Framework* and *Chapter 2, Creating an Opportunity Landscape and Collecting Your Gold Coins*

> ➤ **Your audience and their needs**: We discussed this earlier in the current chapter

> ➤ **Developing key messages for the various audiences**: You can develop this by overlaying your goals and objectives with audience needs

> ➤ **Understanding the various channels of communication available at your disposal**: Understanding the reach and effectiveness of the channels of communication available to you

Based on the preceding list, you need to clearly articulate your communication strategy, which describes which key messages you want to convey to your audience and why, how, and what do you expect to achieve out of this exercise.

Let's take an example to clarify how to build a communication strategy. We shall use the same one from *Chapter 1, Building Your Strategy Framework*, strategic cascade section around an X-ray manufacturer growing its service business in the K-12 schools in tier-1 and tier-2 cities by remotely connecting to the machines, monitoring online performance parameters of the machines, providing predictive diagnostics, and enabling an online expert community of doctors to consult with. For the purpose of this example, we will focus on the internal audience.

There are two groups of existing internal employees who are impacted the most by this initiative—the sales people serving those markets and the service technicians in those cities. There is a new group of employees who will become part of this—the analysts who will be managing the remote monitoring and analysis activities. The information needs for these 3 groups of internal people are as follows:

> ➤ **Sales personnel**: What is the new offering, how to sell it, and how does it impact their performance options and incentives?

> ➤ **Service technicians**: What is the new offering, how reliable is it, and how does it impact their job activities?

> ➤ **Remote analysts**: Why is this new offering critical for the organization, what is their role in the process, and how they should do their jobs?

The key messages for the same set of people can be articulated as follows:

> ➤ **Sales personnel**: The company is bringing a new differentiated service offering enabled by Big Data and remote analytics to the K-12 school market in tier-1 and tier-2 cities that will boost their chances of sales success

> ➤ **Service technicians**: The company is enabling the service technicians in tier-1 and tier-2 cities assisting K-12 school customers with more focused insights and an increased number of service opportunities, both enabled by a robust application of Big Data and remote analytics

> ➤ **Remote analysts**: The company is leveraging Big Data and remote analytics to venture into a new differentiated service business model in the K-12 school markets of tier-1 and tier-2 cities to bring more predictive insights, leading to better equipment maintenance and operation

Notice that the core content of what the company is trying to achieve is the same, but the messages are tweaked a bit to resonate with the information needs of the different groups.

Sales people usually have the propensity to use the latest technology and devices; they are also normally always connected and usually not in office, so using digital media such as e-mails and internal social media will be appropriate to address them. They might be okay to generally understand the concept and process without detailed technical induction. They will also need some training on the new business model and on enabling the ecosystem. This training is best delivered in person.

For service technicians, the actual nature of their job and activities will probably not change much, but they will need a detailed understanding of the remote analytics process and how it will trigger actions for them. They will want to see the system working and possibly review manuals and other documents.

The analysts will need a very detailed understanding of the customer's environment, usage of the equipment, the actual analytics, and the life cycle maintenance process for X-ray machines. They will mostly be confined to the office, so a number of different channels could work for them; however, they will also need a practical demonstration of the machines at field while in use to best relate to what they are analyzing and how their analysis impacts the other stakeholders in the process.

So your strategy, in brief, for these groups of people will develop as follows:

➤ **Sales personnel**: Communicate the power of a new differentiated service offering that will amplify their opportunity landscape using internal media blasts and focused sales training, leading to a higher sales pipeline and increased conversion rate

➤ **Service technicians**: For the new service offering that will enable them to perform better, communicate the robustness of the offering with detailed technical demonstration and documentation, leading to better customer satisfaction and increased business

➤ **Remote analysts**: Communicate the criticality and role of this new service offer and explain the process in detail, from analytical activities to physical maintenance, using practical exposure and detailed documentation, the offering resulting in thought leadership and increased business for the company

Once you are done with the strategy, you will be ready to build your communication plan; we will work on that in the next section. After building the plan, you also need to work on the following:

➤ Devising methods to measure the success of your communication program

➤ Planning methods to adapt your communication plan based on unforeseen progress and feedback

We will suggest some ideas around these topics in the subsequent section.

Building your communication plan

A communication plan is a detailed tactical action outline used to execute your communication strategy. It is important to keep in mind the difference between a strategy and a plan. Strategy revolves around developing the key messages that you want to convey to your audience, and why, how, and what do you expect to achieve out of this exercise. A plan is a tactical design for delivering that strategy. You should involve the communications department of your organization to build this. If you are a small business and do not have a formal communications department, enlist the services or advice of a specialist. Your Big Data strategy and your communication strategy are the two guiding pillars for building the plan, so review them in conjunction before you start the development process.

Your communication plan will comprise many pieces of information, such as the following:

- ➤ Objective
- ➤ Audience
- ➤ Key messages
- ➤ Message delivery format
- ➤ Delivery channel
- ➤ Individual or group delivering the message
- ➤ Schedule of message delivery
- ➤ Expected outcome of the messaging exercise

One objective may have multiple audiences. There may be multiple key messages for each audience for a single objective; list them separately. Each key message may be delivered through multiple formats and channels. However, make sure that for every format and channel, there is a unique responsible person delivering it at a specified time for a desired outcome. Building this plan is a tedious process, but your efforts will be directly proportional to the success of its deployment.

Make a note

The Big Data world is laced with jargon, so avoid them as much as possible in any communication. If you need to use them, explain them thoroughly; you want to avoid people getting confused and distanced from your initiative.

Once you build the plan, we recommend that you follow a few best practices to make it a success:

- ➤ Extensively debate it in your Big Data project team, and get divergent views from the various members; their different perspectives of the project will enrich your plan
- ➤ Get buy-in from your leadership and key stakeholders of the project; their commitment and participation will be critical to take the initiative forward
- ➤ As you roll-out your communication program, publish the key events and highlights upfront to the entire organization; prepare them for what is coming
- ➤ Update the plan frequently, at least once a month or at the end of every key milestone
- ➤ Make the change leader responsible for the administration of this plan

With a robust plan developed, launch your communication campaign with gusto.

Engaging executives effectively

The executive leadership of your business has a very significant role to play in your communication program. If you are one of them, there is extra responsibility on you to make the Big Data program a success. This is imperative because of the following reasons:

- ➤ You want Big Data to be at the front and center in the strategic agenda of your business

- ➤ You do not want your project to be treated like just another technology fad

- ➤ You want people to believe that Big Data and all that you are doing around it is here to stay and will play a considerable role in the future of your business

- ➤ You want the influence of your leaders to rally the people

- ➤ You want them to help tackle any noise that may arise

- ➤ You want them to frame the prospects and possibilities in a very articulate manner to the external world, including your shareholders

- ➤ You want them to sponsor you and steer you

In order to engage your executives effectively, you need to brief them very well just in case they have not been intimately involved with your initiative. Prepare a detailed communication package for them with content that includes material you have prepared for the various audience groups. You also need to provide a crisp summarized version of all that information. Most of your executives are pressed for time, and you need to help them use it wisely. Do not engage them after the fact; keep them in the loop as you progress through your thinking and project work. Their in-process feedback will help you improve the program. Get to know your leaders well and understand their preferences and agenda for growth. Tune your messaging to them so that it appeals to them quickly:

- ➤ For a finance-oriented leader, talk numbers from the start

- ➤ For a more sales-oriented leader, cast your initiative output in terms of the impact on customers and market share

- ➤ For a more operations-oriented leader, talk about the efficiencies and improvement

- ➤ For somebody who is more interested in status quo, discuss how the entire business sustainability will be jeopardized in the absence of your initiative

- ➤ For somebody who is more aggressive about growth, show the possibilities of changing the market and how your business will become the leading player

For all the different executives, you will need to develop a customized briefing. Use their different approaches to reach out effectively to the different demographics in your organization. In most businesses where we have seen Big Data become very successful, the executives in that organization have led the charge from the front.

Monitoring and modulating your communication program

Ultimately, your business results are the best reflection of the effectiveness of your Big Data initiative and all your related communication efforts. However, since this could be a protracted journey, it is best to seek feedback, measure participation, and manage effectiveness as you progress through the stages of the initiative.

Effectiveness metrics

Meanwhile, as you are going through the process, there are many tools and metrics you can use to measure the effectiveness of your communication program. It is important to decide the metrics and plan for collecting the feedback upfront as you venture into developing your communication plan. Some of the popular metrics are as follows:

Percentage outreach

This is the percentage of the audience population your message has reached. Technology today allows the statistics for most of the digital communication platforms to be collected–be it social media or some other kind of online tool. For direct engagement, for example town-hall or small group meetings, you can always rely on attendance. For other channels, tabulating this metric is very difficult; sometimes, companies do surveys to assess this, but they are not very reliable.

Audience engagement

This refers to how much your audience is participating in your communication activities. In cases of social media tools, it is very easy to understand audience engagement based on posts such as comments. For direct engagement, questions asked are a good indication of audience engagement. For other channels, gauging audience engagement is extremely difficult.

Improvement suggestions

This metric is very useful to understand how much the audience (especially internal and external audience groups) has absorbed what you are trying to achieve and how much they are able to relate to it. To collect this type of feedback, ensure there are forums or methods that are very wellpublicized, if required anonymous, and easy to access.

Measuring effectiveness

There are many ways to measure the effectiveness of your communication program. The easiest way is to collect statistics around the pertinent metrics you have chosen. For example, for % outreach, tabulate the distribution through digital logs or attendance sheets; for audience engagement, look at the traffic on digital media platforms and quantity and quality of in-session interactions; for improvement suggestions, account for the valid ones you have chosen to pursue.

Sometimes, an organization considers adherence to the communication plan as a measure of effectiveness. It is a valid choice, but is mostly a lag indicator; the other ones we have talked about are more lead indicators and therefore may be more valuable to measure effectiveness.

Lastly, measuring effectiveness is a process; there are a few best practices we recommend you follow:

> ➤ Continue to collect feedback periodically as your communication program is being rolled out. Do not wait for the end of the program; it might get too late.

> ➤ Share your collected feedback with the audience; this will help them understand what other people are thinking and how they are taking in all the changes.

> ➤ If you take any action on the feedback received, for example changing your messaging or even tweaking your Big Data program, share those with the audience; they will feel valued and become more engaged with your initiative.

> ➤ Monitor the expectations of changed behavior and actions (as a result of your Big Data initiatives) from the various audience groups, and share this with your audience groups.

> ➤ Celebrate success, for success breeds more success; people need to know that things are working and your business is transforming.

Remember there is nothing like adequate communication; the more the merrier.

Summary

About a 100 years back, the famous Irish playwright George Bernard Shaw remarked that "The single biggest problem in communication is the illusion that it has taken place". Often, we venture into business critical projects, share it with our other colleagues, and perceive that everybody is rallied around it. Often, we are wrong, and Big Data initiatives are not immune to this problem; in fact, due to its novel nature, a Big Data project needs more extensive communication. In this final chapter, we have addressed this issue.

We started the chapter with understanding why effective communication is so critical for Big Data projects. Then, we delved into identifying the unique communication needs for various audience groups—internal, external, and shareholders. Famous American entrepreneur and motivational speaker Jim Rohn said, "Effective communication is 20% what you know and 80% what you feel about it". So, it is important that any communication is tailored, considering the background and needs of each different audience group or many of the subgroups that we discussed in this chapter. Your communication exercise needs to be laced with lots of examples, work-out simulations, and what-of scenarios.

Next, we studied the various communication channels and worked on a framework to assess the effectiveness of those channels in the context of your business. Remember to use as many channels as your bandwidth and budget allows, so that the message can reach the maximum possible population in a mode they are most tuned to.

We then built your communication strategy and communication plan. We also discussed how to engage your executives most effectively to lend more credibility to your program, direct greater organizational resources towards your endeavor, and eliminate any noise around the change management program triggered by your Big Data initiative. Finally, we discussed how to analyze and adapt the progress of your communication program. It is critical to keep improvising as you progress so that you can capture the latest needs of your business and people.

Communication is effective when it is converted into actionable knowledge, so to effectively communicate, remember to talk!

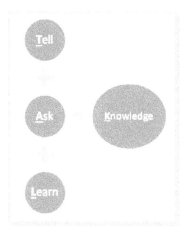

You start by sharing (telling) with people what Big Data is, why your business is invested in this initiative, how things are changing, and what people must do differently in the face of this change. Then, you seek (ask) feedback in the form of actions and interpretations that people have of your Big Data initiative. Finally, you assess (learn) how people are assimilating all about your Big Data initiative through the results and keep modulating your communicating program.

Now, you are all set to venture in the exciting journey of Big Data to transform your business!

www.ingramcontent.com/pod-product-compliance
Lightning Source LLC
LaVergne TN
LVHW081344050326
832903LV00024B/1300